'No tail-enders in this XI. Every essay lyrically evokes the still paradise of summer, the beauty of cricket and why the game matters so much to those of us who can't possibly imagine life without it' Duncan Hamilton

'The Authors' search for the grail should fascinate and amuse anyone with a love for the game' *Daily Telegraph*

'Ingenious ... As with any box of chocolates, there will be flavours you like and one or two orange creams ... The main thing is that Campbell has chosen his team more on writing ability than on cricketing ability. This is the right way round. You may end up losing more games than you win, but the match reports are something else' Marcus Berkmann, *Daily Mail*

'Entertaining and perceptive ... a good innings for all concerned' *Observer*

'A lyrical study underlining again why cricket can stir the soul ... The majority [of pieces] hit the spot like a crisply-struck cover drive' *Scotsman*

'There are solid contributions, stylish cameos and writers who can so deftly craft a sentence like a glorious cover drive that a careless shot or two does not diminish their aura too greatly' *Daily Telegraph*

'Most cricket authors are better at cricket than writing. Reversing this principle is a revelation' Simon Barnes

'The book provides some gently diverting reflections and meanderings to fill those moments when rain stops play' *Country Life*

'A seductive blend of action and reflection, of humour and anecdotage, all underscored by the eternal truth that the memory of a sweetly timed cover drive transcends any amount of flannelled foolishness' David Kynaston

'When it comes to nostalgia value there are few modern sports that can outdo cricket ... an affectionate look at the game and its appeal' *Yorkshire Post*

'Even cricket-sceptics should enjoy a witty and bucolic account of a year in a team featuring Sebastian Faulks and ex-*Downton* star Dan Stevens' Francis Wheen, *Mail on Sunday*

'The delight is in the anecdotes, personalities and fables that make the game ... There are also wonderful nuggets of obscure information ... Read and enjoy, but also ponder the imperilled future of the incomparable game' *Literary Review*

'The Authors battle manfully against the dreadful summer of 2012 ... There is, as might be expected, some terrific writing. Surely only in this book would a bowler's discipline earn the tribute as accurate as a fact-checker on the *New Yorker*' *The Cricketer*

'If you play you'll sympathise with their need for relay fielders to get a throw from the boundary to the wicket ... If you don't you'll still learn a lot. All in all: good areas.' *Spectator*

ABOUT THE AUTHORS CC

They were just one of several literary cricket teams around at the beginning of the twentieth century – famously, J. M. Barrie had his Allahakbarries and P. G. Wodehouse, A. A. Milne and *Punch* all had their own elevens. But the Authors were the only team made up entirely of writers and they would play at Lord's each year, against the Publishers and Actors. Arthur Conan Doyle and Wodehouse once opened the batting. This Authors side played their last match in 1912, losing to the Publishers.

A century on, the Authors are playing again, having been revived by Charlie Campbell and Nicholas Hogg. The new-look side includes brothers Tom and James Holland, William Fiennes and Alex Preston, professional-cricketer-turned-author Ed Smith and historians Matthew Parker and Thomas Penn.

Follow them on Twitter at @AuthorsCC

THE AUTHORS XI

THE AUTHORS XI

A Season of English Cricket from Hackney to Hambledon

The Authors Cricket Club

BLOOMSBURY

LONDON · NEW DELHI · NEW YORK · SYDNEY

First published in Great Britain 2013

This paperback edition published 2014

Copyright © by the Authors Cricket Club 2013

The moral right of the authors has been asserted

No part of this book may be used or reproduced in any manner
whatsoever without written permission from the Publisher except in
the case of brief quotations embodied in critical articles or reviews.

Every reasonable effort has been made to trace copyright holders of
material reproduced in this book, but if any have been inadvertently
overlooked the publishers would be glad to hear from them.

John Wisden & Co.
An imprint of Bloomsbury Publishing Plc
50 Bedford Square, London WC1B 3DP

www.wisden.com
www.bloomsbury.com

Bloomsbury is a trademark of Bloomsbury Publishing Plc

Bloomsbury Publishing, London, New Delhi, New York and Sydney

A CIP catalogue record for this book is available from the British Library

ISBN 978 1 4088 4047 4

10 9 8 7 6 5 4 3 2 1

Typeset in Garamond by Saxon Graphics Ltd, Derby
Printed and bound in Great Britain by CPI Group (UK) Ltd,
Croydon CR0 4YY

CONTENTS

FOREWORD

You'd have thought that a cricket team that had been defunct for a hundred years should be allowed to rest in peace. So when Charlie Campbell and Nicholas Hogg said they wanted to resurrect an Authors XI based on the one founded by, among others, Arthur Conan Doyle and P. G. Wodehouse before the First World War, it seemed, at best, a quixotic idea. Authors are fantasists; they may know a lot about cricket, but few of them are any good at it. The Edinburgh doctor Conan Doyle was more of a rugby man; Wodehouse was short-sighted; and for their twenty-first-century successors I could foresee a long and embarrassing summer.

Yet less than a year later, there we were on the waterfront in Mumbai in a day/night match against Osian's CC – not winning, but giving them a run for their money, thanks to a 62-ball century from children's author Joe Craig, stepping away to leg and flat-batting in a one-day style that might have caused Jeeves to raise an eyebrow one sixteenth of an inch. The day before, we had had a Bombay Gymkhana team in serious trouble at 18 for 5 until they sent for their heavy guns. There followed a game in Jodhpur that we really should have won and an amazing encounter in the desert against a village called Rohet. This too we might have won had it not been for a fine batsman imported from one of Jodhpur's top clubs who took a fancy to the literary attack. Their bowlers were village lads who had got up at four a.m. to work so they could be free for the two o'clock start. I asked one how often he played. 'Three times a week, twelve months a year,' he said. 'No close season.'

Our final game was against a Rajasthan Royals Eleven in Jaipur, as a curtain-raiser for the literature festival. We were welcomed by elephants, men on huge stilts, dancing girls and drummers; Charlie Campbell went out to toss riding on a camel. His opposing captain was the Indian Test bowler Sreesanth. We were deep into fantasy country here, though this did not stop us tensely checking on the protective equipment in the dressing room. Sreesanth's opening partner was meant to be the 100-mph Shaun Tait of Australia. We had brought only two helmets and an insufficient number of boxes. In the event, the day could not have been more friendly: Taity had missed his plane and Sreesanth bowled leg spin. We lost, but once again did not disgrace ourselves.

The Authors – we had in any case decided one chilly night in the tents of desert Rajasthan – are a side better suited to the three-day game. It was one of those bonding moments that happen when a certain amount of beer has been drunk on successive nights. Was there some post-modern irony in the relish with which these learned historians and avant-garde novelists accepted their laddish nicknames – Prof, Bearders, Biggles? Not that you would have noticed. The best such name was gifted to us by an enthusiastic young man in old Jodhpur. In a backstreet, he approached Ngayu Thairu, our photographer, all-rounder and trainee colorectal specialist, and asked if he could practise his English on him. All right, said Ngayu. As his name implies, Ngayu is Kenyan. You should also know that he is not particularly tall. He was therefore surprised when the young Indian told him he reminded him of someone he had seen on British television. Ten excited minutes later he finally recalled the name: John Cleese. And so the nickname 'Cleesey' came to be.

The Indian tour was unforgettable, but what mattered most to the Authors XI was the full summer programme in England, which is described in the pages that follow. If there was a degree of luck that so many decent cricketers were free enough from other club ties to give so much time to a new team, there was also a good deal of organisation and persuasion to make it so. What strikes me as remarkable is that all the players are genuinely authors; the captain has resisted the lure of vaguely literary ringers to strengthen the side. And in any event, the best eleven, which would sadly not include this author, needs no stiffening to match a good village or Sunday club side.

The pieces that follow reveal a good deal about their writers as well as about their subjects. Amateur cricketers tend to be vain, anecdotal, passionate, knowledgeable, neurotic and given to fantasy. So do writers. The game is made for the profession. Will you pick up the little undercurrents of rivalry, the small resentments, as well as the friendship and the deep love of the game?

I don't know; but I can say for sure that if you enjoy these pages half as much as I enjoyed playing with their authors, then you are in for a treat.

Sebastian Faulks

INTRODUCTION
Charlie Campbell

On 29 June 1905, P. G. Wodehouse and Arthur Conan Doyle opened the batting for the original Authors side. They made an unlikely pair striding out on to the green sward of Lord's. Wodehouse was at the beginning of his literary career, having only left the Hong Kong & Shanghai Bank three years previously, and was awestruck to be opening with his literary hero, Conan Doyle, who was then at the peak of his fame. Wodehouse had spent two seasons in the Dulwich 1st XI (1899 and 1900), as a myopic fast bowler and number eleven batsman; Conan Doyle was a formidable all-rounder, who'd turned out for the MCC ten times and, famously, was said to have had W. G. Grace caught at the wicket with a long hop.

The creators of the superhuman Jeeves and Sherlock Holmes were not quite the men of steel and reason you might expect. Conan Doyle almost abandoned his most famous creation and his medical practice to write books about spiritualism (from a believer's perspective); and Wodehouse fans are well used to having to defend their beloved author for his stupid and naive wartime broadcasts from Nazi Germany. The two writers were united by a love of cricket and each wrote about unlikely sporting heroes – perhaps influenced by their matches for the Authors at Lord's. Conan Doyle's 'The Story of Spedegue's Dropper' relates how an asthmatic, short-sighted schoolteacher practised his lob bowling in the New Forest, the ball soaring over a rope tied between two trees, before descending upon the stumps at an uncommon velocity. Spedegue was fast-tracked into the national side and became England's unlikely Ashes hero, with this unplayable ball. Meanwhile, Wodehouse's *Psmith in the City* saw Mike Jackson leave his desk at the bank in which he worked, speeding over to Lord's to play for Middlesex, after a minor prang (in Wodehouse speak) left them a player short for their match against Surrey. Needless to say, he makes a century and can leave the world of finance behind at the most famous ground in the world.

The Authors had emerged out of J. M. Barrie's Allahakbarries, who were one of several occasional literary teams of the time (very charmingly portrayed in Kevin Telfer's *Peter Pan's First XI*), but they were a better side. Barrie never played at Lord's, being a moderate player by his own admission. He was a slow bowler who said that if he didn't like a ball, he'd run after it, stop it and bowl it again. And his team took after him, being comprised of writers, artists, explorers and a Frenchman who'd never played cricket before. They practised mostly on the train to matches. One player confidently declared that 'intellect always tells in the end' but this was rarely the case.

The modern-day Authors started out along similar lines. In 1981, Australian captain Kim Hughes dismissed his Ashes counterpart Mike Brearley saying that 'he had nothing going for him except that he was intelligent'. This is truer of us than it was of Brearley, who was a fine batsman, if not quite of the highest class. And so we adopted it as our motto, once it had been translated into Latin – *Praeter Ingenium Nihil* – by the team's resident classicist, Tom Holland.

The idea for the team originated in the summer of 2011, when I was asked to put together a side of writers to play against a bank. The word got out that we needed suitable recruits and Nicholas Hogg got in touch. Nick had a proper cricket pedigree, having played for Leicestershire at youth level. While his team-mate Darren Maddy went on to play for England, Nick chose the novelist's path over that of the professional sportsman. He and I spent the rest of the summer travelling from match to match. It was after the last game – played in the rain on a pitch next to the M25 and under power lines – as we contemplated the bleak cricketless months ahead that the idea came to us of putting together a team of writers to play the perfect season. We would play a range of fixtures, at some of the most spectacular grounds in the country – maybe even Lord's if we were lucky.

The original Authors had played their last match there in 1912 against the Actors, in one of the wettest summers ever recorded. Play was suspended after that for some time, as this golden age of wandering cricket came to an end. C. Aubrey Smith, the Actors' captain and one-Test wonder, moved to Los Angeles, where he founded the Hollywood Cricket Club. Wodehouse was its first secretary and Boris Karloff kept wicket. There have been a few incarnations of the Authors since then. One, in the 1950s, featured Douglas Jardine, Jack Fingleton and Len Hutton in the line-up, with a handful of writers batting down the order. But, a century after the last match at Lord's, we reverted to the original literary ideal, with Ed Smith as the solitary former professional in the side. He was joined by a number of novelists, historians, children's authors, and an actor and publisher, from our traditional rivals.

Writers are not always good sportsmen, usually aren't in fact. Nor were we a young team, since publication happens more frequently in one's later years. (Not only is Amol Rajan the youngest national newspaper editor in the country, but he is also the youngest Author.) But in our first season, we defied creaking limbs to play fifteen games. It might have been the rainiest summer since 1912 but we were remarkably fortunate, losing only our match at Arundel Castle to the elements.

Wodehouse's first paid writing commission was a piece on sporting captaincy. This was a subject of which he had little experience but he didn't let that concern him and pocked half a guinea for his troubles. At the outset, my captaincy experience was similarly limited. I had a car, which counts for a lot at this level of cricket, when many of my team-mates don't even have a driving licence. My day job is as a literary agent, so organising cricket for writers and driving them around has come reasonably naturally. The Allahakbarries had an agent in their squad – Addison Bright handled J. M. Barrie's theatrical affairs. But in 1906 it transpired that he had embezzled £28,000 from his fellow cricketers (including £16,000 from Barrie and £9,000 from Conan Doyle). He fled to Switzerland where he shot himself.

We needed to improve on this business model. Nick and I asked our team-mates to write chapters for this book about our season. The idea was that each chapter would focus on an aspect of cricket, and feature a match report, as we played a suitable opposition. So historian Matthew Parker would write about cricket and empire as we played the East London Community XI in Hackney. Tom Holland, always on the verge of giving up cricket completely, would tackle the subject of ageing, as we played a strong team of teenagers. His brother James Holland had done what so many of us yearned to do, building his own beautiful ground in Wiltshire. He would write about that, as we played Tim Rice's Heartaches. Other chapters fell into line easily. Kamila Shamsie was given – not very originally perhaps as the sole female player – the fixture against Shepperton Ladies. William Fiennes, author of *The Snow Geese*, would cover the match at the Valley of Rocks, surely one of the most scenic pitches in the world. Amol

Rajan would take on the Establishment as we played the Tory-heavy Lords and Commons CC at John Paul Getty's spectacular ground at Wormsley. Anthony McGowan would focus on cricket and class, as we played at Harold Larwood's old club, aiming much of his wit at his own team-mates. And Ed Smith and Dan Stevens would write of sport and drama as we played we would play against a side of Actors on the ultimate stage of all, Lord's.

The Authors might never rival Spedegue or Mike Jackson's fictional achievements but Conan Doyle's dismissal of W. G. Grace with a rank ball was within our grasp. Cricket can provide those moments of sporting joy, when amateur and professional can share the field and, fleetingly, forget the chasm that separates them. In 2013 alone, we faced Sreesanth and his team-mates from the Rajasthan Royals; we defeated the national team of Japan, who were ranked 37th in the world; and we won against a charity side starring Mark Ramprakash and Devon Malcolm. The fastest England bowler of recent times rolled back the years, genially bouncing Sam Carter, and Ramps scored yet another stunning century, but somehow it was them presenting us with man-of-the-match awards at the end. We were still thrashed by Kirkby Portland though. Some things never change.

NETS

Peter Frankopan

Building the Authors XI

By and large, authors do not like the moving image as a medium. Before Kindles and ebooks emerged from the digital bushes to draw fire, films were the unspoken enemy. The knowing glances and the hint of a pout; the misty eyes that do not quite break into a tear; the disbelief at unexpected news. Easy to capture on camera. And while not impossible to capture in prose, difficult – and difficult to do well: for one thing you need to avoid phrases like 'knowing glances' and 'misty eyes'.

Historians dislike Kindles intensely. The footnotes. Where are the footnotes? And why are they so hard to use? But they dislike films even more, at least when they are about their special subject. *Kingdom of Heaven* with Orlando Bloom? I could barely speak for two days. *Ivanhoe* with Anthony Andrews – still gives me sleepless nights. *A Knight's Tale* – now I'm starting to sound sour.

But I defy even the most considered and erudite scholar of the Second World War to have a bad word about the best war film of all time, and the template for how to assemble everything from a team of misfit assassins, to – well – a team of cricket-playing authors: *The Dirty Dozen*.

One by one, trucks decant hardened criminals, each one introduced with the length of sentence he is serving: thirty years' imprisonment; twenty years' hard labour; thirty years' hard labour; twenty years' imprisonment; death by hanging. All are loners and dropouts, each one uncomfortable in the presence of other men: they are too used to assessing their peers for potential weaknesses, and ready at the slightest provocation to throw a punch in self-defence. Some can even hear voices.

As the Authors gathered at Edgbaston[1] for the first meeting, the first nets session (bowling machines, video analysis – the lot), the similarities were unmistakable. Each arrived one by one, short pleasantries mixed by the common knowledge that we had been recruited for a specific mission – a mission that offered freedom from our own sentences: twenty years already served on medieval Greek literature and the First Crusade;[2] imminent release from the origins of Islam;[3] parole from *Winter King*;[4] hard labour on *Einstein's Underpants*;[5] solitary confinement for *The Music Room*;[6] the cell door flung open from transatlantic love.[7]

Because writing can be like prison: solitary; humourless; silent; the thought of publication the only spur to get through the long, dark nights when no one can hear you talking to yourself. On a bad day, the desk is a cell from which you can move but cannot escape; when the mocking of the blinking cursor challenging you to express thoughts and ideas – or, worst of all, facts! – feels like a sadistic guard laughing, jangling keys as you sit motionless and unproductive.

---

1   The actual Edgbaston – venue for Test matches, one-day internationals and home of Warwickshire County Cricket Club.
2   P. J. A. Frankopan.
3   T. Holland.
4   T. D. Penn.
5   A. J. McGowan.
6   W. J. Fiennes.
7   N. A. Hogg.

So there we were, offered an escape from penance not just for the day, but with the promise of repeated release during the summer for a season of matches that we were almost obliged to play in, games where we could not be at our desk because we were forced to be outside. We were a cricketing Dirty Dozen.

So, the dance of strangers. Who knew each other already, and who was new? Whose books had you read and whose books should you have read? How much cricket had you played, and how much better were you when you were young and fit, when your eyesight was actually not that bad? Were wisecracks a sign of nerves and a desire to be accepted or the way to cement a place in the team? And what of our Lee Marvin – captain Charlie Campbell? Would he lead from the front as a strong, silent type, or mix things up as one of the boys?

But first came the nervous exchanges as we were forced into physical conditioning by Darren Maddy[8] and Neil Carter[9] – squat thrusts; sprints; muscle flexes. I was glad results were not being plotted on a graph. But I was also glad that I did know rules one, two and three for meeting new comrades at arms; don't sweat, don't breathe too deeply and don't look tired by the warm-up. We were told to run towards a trampoline to perfect the jump before delivery; it was harder than it sounds. Some never made it. We took part in drills to take the perfect diving slip catch, only to bang heads as two went for the same ball. Then competition time: drop it and you're out. Ah, the school drill: look like it's just a game, but strain every sinew to be last man standing. And, sure enough, there was one left at the end, clutching the ball. They must like me now: validation.

8   D. W. Maddy, ex-England Test and one-day international, ex-Leicestershire; current Warwickshire. RHB; twenty-six first-class centuries; terrific hand–eye coordination; astonishing core body strength.

9   N. M. Carter, Warwickshire. LHB; LFM over the wicket; 297 first-class wickets.

Over the weeks that followed, as players gathered from all corners of the publishing and writing worlds, a unit slowly but surely began to take shape, a team ready to defy the odds. Fresh, new faces appeared at our next nets sessions at Lord's. A sense of a team was developing. The swell in numbers was almost as comforting as the arrival of talent – stand-tall batsmen,[10] wristy spinners,[11] elegant shotmakers,[12] buccaneering virtuosi[13] and a wicketkeeper whose glove work was matched by his wit.[14] And there was more to come: a superstar writer, whose name alone would strike fear into the opposition.[15] Nor was I, it turned out, the only international cricketer up for selection.[16]

As I worked away over the summer, battling against a new history of Russia, Persia and Central Asia and urging my fingers on to tap at the keys of my laptop, I secretly strained, waiting for emails to come in revealing when and where the next nets session and game would be. My kitbag, long used to holding court at the back of the luggage cupboard, started to get used to sitting by the front door, and even taking up residence in the boot of the car. Invitations to play at other games (for other teams – shh!) were gleefully accepted. But my conditioning was all being saved for the Authors CC.

Sprung from the purgatory of once having been actually quite good but with boots long hanging sorrowful and unused, the challenge was to keep up with a team that was beginning to upgrade its aims and ambitions. There was whispered talk of the possibility of a season unbeaten; of games against those whose

---

10 S. M. Carter.
11 M. Waheed.
12 J. Holland.
13 A. J. Rajan.
14 A. H. M. Preston†.
15 S. C. Faulks.
16 E. T. Smith, ex-England Test international, Cambridge University, Kent, Middlesex; RHB, thirty-four first-class centuries; P. J. A. Frankopan, RHB, ex-Croatia one-day international; no first-class centuries (or half-centuries).

scalps could be displayed if we could take them. No longer the Dirty Dozen, it was more like Greek heroes gathering at Troy. It was no longer a question of which of us was the indolent dropout but which was our Achilles (Carter); not who was the unstable liability, but who had hair as lustrous as Menelaus (too close to call between Stevens and Campbell). Whose exploits would end in glorious triumph (a now internationally-famous six by Holland T.) or heart-breaking tragedy (there is one over that I bowled in the Lord's game that I sincerely hope does not feature in this book).

Sadly, the other teams were too well behaved, too polite at clapping us on and off the field, too gracious in victory and too friendly in defeat for Tolkien to provide the cast of characters that our enemies resembled or that we could emulate. Also, the fact that there was no ring does not help.

But the season was in one way a quest. A quest for a team to form, for players to get used to each other. I'm still not sure how it all turned out to be such a success and such fun. I have my suspicions, though, that the all-for-one and one-for-all attitude had something to do with the selfless decisions of the captain[17] and vice-captain[18] to model their facial hair on that of D'Artagnan and Aramis respectively.

And so, greetings over, introductions made, training done, kit polished and upgraded for the first time in more than a decade, it was time to find out exactly what we were made of. As the French revolutionaries shouted to each other to prepare: *Aux armes!* And as it happens, that is exactly the cry you need on the cricket field. Shout it loudly enough in French and, to the cricketer's ear, it is unmistakable: Howzat!

17 C. A. MacA. Campbell*.
18 N. A. Hogg.

After the intensity of our nets session, it was time for our season to begin in earnest. Our game against the ELCCC would, we believed, be the Authors' first match in a hundred years. We approached this historic fixture with excitement, selecting an experienced side for our trip to Hackney. But we subsequently uncovered several later incarnations of our writers' side – one of which featured Douglas Jardine and Len Hutton. Our own former England player wasn't available for this game – but at various points during the season, it did feel as if our opponents had selected their strongest side in the expectation of playing against him.

EMPIRE STATE OF MIND
Matthew Parker

Authors XI vs ELCCC, 22 April, Victoria Park

> *Cricket civilises people and creates good gentlemen.*
>
> Robert Mugabe

I t's all bloody nerve-racking. I'm organising our first ever fixture as a newly revived team. There's been a stream of phone calls and emails between me and Iqbal Miah, the secretary of our opposition, the East London Community Cricket Club, amid much doubt that we can get a pitch in our local Victoria Park. It's not certain that the footballers who use it in the winter have actually cleared off, and there are rumours that much of the space is going to be given over to London 2012. 'Don't get me wrong, I love the Olympics,' writes Iqbal in one email, 'but when it infringes on us playing our beautiful beloved game of cricket then that is simply not on.' But eventually a pitch is rented from the council (cost £41), and now we just have the weather to worry about. The forecast is terrible. As originator of the fixture, I feel horribly responsible for everything.

What, for instance, will the Authors (more than half of whom I've met only once or not at all) make of the opposition (and them of us)? Or of our scruffy area, and the artificial pitch? So many of the later fixtures for this Authors XI season are fabulously high-end, historic or stunning – Lord's, Eton, Wormsley, the Valley of Rocks.

As I supervise a child-labour bagel production line at home on the morning of the game – salt beef, smoked salmon, cream cheese – the emails and texts are still pinging about. Apparently our publisher is coming to the match, and our photographer, Ngayu. Suddenly we learn that there is another team expecting to play the ELCCC at the same time. It's double-booked! Iqbal graciously lets the other lot down. We're still on, though the skies are darkening.

To add to the stress, it's about this time for me before a match that the butterflies always set in. As a bowler, I never know quite how it is going to come out – fast, slow, full toss or short – and there is always the ghastly spectre of the 'yips', when for some reason everything goes so wrong you can't even land it on the wicket. I've been struck once, and never want to be again. At this point, when better cricketers might be planning a glorious triumph, I'm just hoping to avoid humiliation.

I've played before with the captain, Charlie, and the two historian Toms, Holland and Penn. We are all about the same level, so that's reassuring. But a nets session or two revealed that there are some much better players in the Authors XI. It's certainly going to be a higher standard than my usual occasional team, Tom Holland's Gents XI (which has been known to field players who have actually never played cricket before). This will be a bit more full on, I think. The butterflies respond and I can't smear mustard on salt beef any longer.

With tea assembled, I gather up my notebook and Dictaphone, to make a record of the game. I borrow a huge *Top of the Pops* *c.*1980-style microphone off my Karaoke-loving son to plug into the incongruously tiny recorder. Kitbag, cold box, extra jumper, large umbrella. We're ready and on our way.

****

Victoria Park, first opened in 1845, is peopled by all sorts, from yummy mummies to hard-as-nails gangsters, who use the low-hanging branches of the trees to 'train' their fighting dogs. At places it is edged by million-pound terraced houses, at others by housing estates with severe challenges. It was originally designated a much-needed play area for poor children from Hackney and Tower Hamlets. (The latter has recently won the uncoveted title of the new child poverty capital of the UK.)

At weekends it is busy with sport – tennis, bowling, endless jogging and in the winter football, and the summer cricket. And then there are the nets. There has to be actual snow on the ground for the nets not to be at least partially occupied every weekend. If all three are full or you're short of players, you just join in with people already in action. Compliments and advice are handed out to everyone; the chat is loud, sharp and funny. And the 'hideously diverse' Britain that regularly turns up would have a *Daily Mail* leader writer frothing – absolutely every age, race, background and income group is represented, all different in so many ways but sharing a huge passion – cricket. If someone had planned for the area's very different communities to get together and get to know each other, they couldn't have done it better.

So this is where this fixture came from. Some of the most regular netters were players from the ELCCC, a mainly Asian team with a few Afro-Caribbeans and others thrown in. But not every East End community is represented at the nets (and very few women, my nine-year-old daughter – good eye, poor technique – aside). You have blokes of South Asian, Afro-Caribbean and English descent; there's often an Aussie or a Kiwi. Of course, the reason for the absence of, say, Turkish or Somali enthusiasts is simple: they managed to avoid being in the British Empire. Does this blatant link to our uncomfortable past spoil the warm glow of the fraternisation at the nets? Is cricket's blatantly imperial history a source of shame, or of celebration?

In 1900, Lord Selbourne, Under-Secretary of State for the Colonies, declared at a dinner for a West Indian touring party that it was impossible to exaggerate the importance of cricket to 'our Imperial unity ... in harmonising and consolidating the different parts of the Empire'. Cricket is, without doubt, the matchlessly imperial game. At its highest level it has only ever been played between England, her colonies or her former colonies. Right up until 1965, the ICC, the sport's governing body, was the *Imperial* Cricket Council. But more than that, cricket is drenched in the ideology and history of the empire, and is still shaped by the empire's legacy in Britain and around the world. Even – perhaps, especially – here in Victoria Park.

As the empire reached its zenith in the late Victorian and early Edwardian period, the epic levels of violence, exploitation and coercion, although largely undiminished, became a bit of an embarrassment to liberals back at home and fuel for a growing number of external and internal critics. Suddenly, a justification was needed for how a small number of British whites ruled over millions in India, Africa and the Caribbean. So apologists for empire now claimed that the enterprise was an exercise in morality, that its expansion had brought 'civilisation, the Christian religion, order, justice'. Importantly, it was the character of the Englishman that 'gives him the right to rule which no other can possess'.

This 'character' was seen at the time as the result of white racial superiority, but also of what C. L. R. James would call 'the public school code'. Taken together, this made the elite white Englishman a natural and benign ruler. The 'public school code' was focused not on academic achievement, but on sport. As the headmaster of Harrow declared at the end of the nineteenth century, 'learning, however excellent in itself, does not afford much necessary scope for such virtues as promptitude, resource, honour, co-operation, and unselfishness; but these are the soul of English games'.

At the heart and 'soul' of this code was cricket. For Victorians, moral worth was found in tradition and history – and cricket already had plenty of both, being the oldest continuous team sport in the country. Furthermore, cricket was inexorably linked to a particularly rural vision of the past that the Victorians liked celebrating – the village green with local inn, soft green hills in the distance – a million miles from the sins and corruption of the cities (where most people already lived). That conditions of grass, ground and sky are important for the game of course contributes to the pastoral colouring (and links it to the Victorian cult of gardening). Allied to this, and part of cricket's aspirational appeal, were the aristocratic rhythms of the game, taking a huge amount of time, interspersed with plenty of breaks for eating, relaxing, drinking and socialising.

But best of all for apologists of empire, cricket was considered to have higher levels of sportsmanship than other games. Cricket, it was proposed, uniquely promoted qualities such as fair play, selflessness, putting the team before the individual, and, perhaps crucially, accepting the decisions of captains and umpires, of authority, without complaint, even if they were wrong. Even today, the MCC website declares that cricket's unique appeal is its 'spirit', which it defines as an adherence to fair play, courtesy, authority and the rules.

In the late Victorian and early Edwardian period, cricket came to encapsulate the spirit of England and how the English, particularly the richer half, viewed their national identity, at the same time becoming a primary justifier and facilitator of empire. For one thing, cricket and its values of sportsmanship told white Englishmen something nice about themselves – that they had the moral authority to rule over other races and could be trusted to do so in a decent manner. It also served as a demonstration of English qualities, sufficient, it was hoped, to convince the colonised to accept the benefits of British rule and aspire to cricket's example of 'pluck and nerve, and self-restraint' (as Cecil Headlam wrote, after a tour of India in 1903).

Perhaps the apogee of the imperial cricketer can be found in the person of George, Lord Harris. Son of an imperial governor, he was born in Trinidad, then grew up in Madras. After Eton and Oxford, he played for Kent, becoming in 1879 the second ever captain of the English Test cricket team. From the House of Lords he was Under-Secretary of State for India, and then for War, until becoming Governor of Bombay in 1890. Harris believed that cricket was a gift from God, and saw England's imperial mission as educating 'oriental people on western lines, to imbue them with western modes of thought'. He maintained that cricket had 'done more to consolidate the Empire than any other influence', and spent virtually all his time promoting the game as part of a culture designed to create a class of pliant Indians mimicking Englishmen and devoted to the empire.

For Harris, cricket was all: he ignored famine, riots and sectarian unrest. When, in 1893, serious interracial conflict broke out in Bombay, he was away from the city watching cricket up country. He did not return until nine days later, and that was only because there was a cricket match in the city he wanted to see. He was widely disliked, and on his departure in 1895 he was described by a local paper as Bombay's worst governor for more than a hundred years. He returned to England to become President of the MCC, and remained a key figure in early twentieth-century cricket.

Lord Harris didn't think much of the Indian cricketers he came across. Though they 'have a good eye and rather long arms,' he declared, 'they do not possess the patience and resolution of the Anglo-Saxon. They are very easily excited.' Indeed, the racist stereotypes that had proved useful in justifying slavery and empire transferred effortlessly to the cricket pitch. Players from the eastern empire were weak, 'too lazy', devious and crooked. (One Parsee player, it was reported, had batted three times for his team through the use of complicated disguises.) West Indians were seen by the white cricket establishment as childlike, volatile, excitable. Even when West Indian players became more familiar in England in the late 1920s and 1930s, their failings were often described as a result of their race. Thus Jack Hobbs in his 1931 autobiography described the 'chief characteristic' of black West Indian cricketers as 'temperament – very high up in the air one minute, very down in the mouth the next. They were just big boys. Which explains why they bowled fast and could not play slow bowling. All boys want to bowl fast.' Neville Cardus agreed, writing that the 'erratic quality of West Indian cricket is surely true to racial type'.

Familiarity, of course, is the best antidote to stereotyping, and cricket, to its credit, did engineer otherwise unlikely mixing between far-flung peoples of the empire – with Aboriginal, Parsee and West Indian teams touring England from 1868 onwards – and within the colonies of the empire, where, although teams were often segregated, they did at least play each other. Touring parties of Englishmen had matches against white, mixed race and entirely Asian teams. Then, from the turn of the century, small numbers of Asian or West Indian players started appearing in County sides. One was exceptional: Prince Ranjitsinhji, born in Sarodar, India, in 1872, who turned out for Cambridge then Sussex, becoming the leading batsman in English cricket, playing fifteen times for England. He had a brilliant eye and great coordination, hitting the ball very late and defying English convention by exploiting the leg side (he was credited with inventing the leg glance).

Ranjitsinhji was a public supporter of empire (many years later he said he had 'tried his best to play with a straight bat for

the Empire') but as the historian of Indian cricket Mihir Bose
has written, his 'strong romantic image ... of an Indian
conquering the English cricket field ... played an important part
in fostering Indian pride and self-respect', which in turn helped
increase support for political independence from Britain. In the
same way, Michael Manley sees the success of George Headley,
'a black man superior at cricket to whites', as boosting the self-
belief of poor African-Caribbeans, challenging white hegemony
on the islands and underwriting support between the wars for
trade unions, wider suffrage, Marcus Garvey's campaign for
black rights, and the strikes of 1938 that are now seen as the
crucible of the West Indian independence movements. So while
at once a sort of imperial crowd control (a Jamaican cricketing
friend of mine called it 'oppression'), cricket, by raising black
confidence, was central in the struggles for decolonisation and
political emancipation. Lord Harris, who died aged eighty-one
in 1932, would have been appalled. It was almost as if cricket –
long deployed as imperial 'soft power', described as 'the grand
Imperial game' – was now turning round to bite the hand that
created it.

****

After much lurching and stumbling, we – me and Ollie, the more
cricket-oriented son – arrive at the 'ground'. It's far from clear
where we are playing or what the hell is going on. Eventually, we
hook up with some familiar faces from the opposition and are
directed to our pitch, one of about six on a large expanse of open
ground at the east end of the park. Although other games are
readying for action, it doesn't seem like a cricket scene, and not
just because of the tower blocks and looming Canary Wharf
skyscrapers, not far away between the trees to the south-east. It's
so early in the season that many of the trees are still without leaf,
the sky is heavy and cold and the wind is bracing.

But there are the players! Straggling groups burdened by huge cricket bags, the odd individual, trying to work out possible Authors XI team-mates. The 'pavilion' is firmly shut up, but there are unlocked toilets, so we get changed there. As we all assemble, everyone seems excited by the Authors project, and thrilled to be included. I identify Tony, whose children's books my kids have enjoyed, and Amol, whose history of spin bowling was among my Christmas presents last year. Amol is the one non-white person on our team. The opposition has a single white person, like a mirror of us.

Then, at last, we are underway. Nick bowls the first over. He's quick and accurate. Then I'm on and – relief! – it comes out okay. Their number one – Shakeel (whose cricketing hero, I discover, is Shakib al Hasan) looks pretty handy – he seems to have plenty of time to play. The other opener, Marcus, is more hesitant, and pretty soon gives a sitter of a catch. But it's dropped! And then there's another one, and another … but with each fumbled chance, the mood of the team lightens in sympathy for the embarrassment of our team-mate, and relief that if it happens to us next, we won't be the only ones. With the outfield so recently gouged about by footballers, fielding is extra difficult. But after an age, wickets start to fall. Iqbal, the opposition's captain, comes out to umpire, and starts heckling and sledging his own batsmen. We get louder and chattier, with Amol leading the way. We start to feel like a team.

Nonetheless, it is clear that we are of varied abilities, to put it mildly. You could even say we are a mixture of Proper Cricketers and Imaginary Cricketers. Proper Cricketers are good at all sports, and have decent coordination and fitness. They can field, rather than letting the ball pass through them as if they were made of air. At least half of their catching chances are safely taken. They probably play league cricket and were in their school's 1st XI. Imaginary Cricketers came to the game late, were never coached;

they roll over in their minds the perfect cover drive or nuanced-but-deadly over, but in reality they miss the ball a lot and spend each delivery trying to correct the imperfections of the last.

More than anything, Proper Cricketers can throw. You either 'have an arm' or you don't. It's the great divider. While opening bowler Nick and opening batter Sam can deliver it from the farthest boundary to the top of the stumps, others like myself require a humiliating halfway man to scoop up our feeble throws and pass them on to the 'keeper or bowler. On a couple of occasions, Sam shouts 'Leave it!' to the bowler in the hope that his arrow of a throw won't be impeded on its way to hitting the stumps. I wonder if his ilk will get frustrated by the standards of their team-mates as the season goes on; I hope the relative inadequacies of the rest of us won't prove too dispiriting.

They're now assaulting our bowling, with their numbers four and five unleashing a series of huge shots. Tom Penn, fielding his own bowling, gets a nasty injury when the ball pops up off the ground into his eye. Tom traipses off bleeding heavily and shocked. 'What's this pitch?!' he shouts. 'What kind of groundsman is it anyway!?' I'm by his side, proffering ice and feeling responsible, and now look around the darkening park, thinking, but not saying, 'Groundsman? Don't they just mow the grass?'

By the time the forty overs are up, they've got more than 250. It seems daunting, and now rain looks imminent. Tea is eaten standing up as there are no chairs, and it's too cold to sit on the ground or keep still. I take the chance to ask some of the opposition how they got into cricket. Amazingly, they all come up with exactly the same answer: 'my dad'.

My own case is a bit different. On a handful of occasions, my dad took me and my sister to the local rec just down the road, and we set up two sets of stumps and bails. He tried to teach us to play but didn't get far. It's no use having just three players, and there was no discernible talent. My dad, although cricket was very much his favourite sport, was not a great one for pursuing something just for the fun of it, rather than winning, so he didn't push it.

All I remember from cricket at school is being bored and thirsty in the outfield. It tended to be two or three boys with obvious talent who did all the bowling and batting and monopolised the attention of the coaches. The rest of us were there to make up the numbers. A couple of visits to Test matches with my dad failed to excite any enthusiasm. It just seemed like a load of old buffers in jackets and ties, polite chit-chat, tinkling wine glasses, the occasional rueful joke about how terrible England were. (For people of my dad's generation, the steady, all-too-evident decline of English cricket was perhaps a natural thing, a cosy, tinted reflection of the startlingly fast collapse of the empire during the same period. Somehow, it was even *right*. When, at the end of his life, England achieved number one Test status, it threw my dad completely.)

Even the heroics of 1981, when I was eleven, passed me by. Cricket, I felt, was stuffy, old-fashioned, Establishment, elitist. That whole Lord's/Henley/Wimbledon thing was just the worst. As soon as I could, I gave up playing completely. Then, when I was thirteen, my dad was posted with Shell to Barbados, and everything changed.

Barbados was strange. A beautiful paradise of sand, sea and sun, of course, but also uneasy and unreal: a tiny island with so many people, created by some terrible history, and now totally reliant on tourism – white people at leisure being served drinks by black waiters.

Perhaps the fact that my sister and I only came out from boarding school in England for the holidays contributed for us to the sense of unreality. We were never part of it. We only mixed with the children of other expatriates or of the stream of family friends who came to stay. I can't say we ever had any black friends, which I now find rather strange and sad.

For my dad it was a dream job. In those days Shell sponsored the inter-island cricket, so much of his time was taken up watching matches. He was the white guy in a suit who gave out the cheques at the end. It also meant the pick of Test match tickets, and for the visit of Australia to the island in March 1984, he got me a seat right behind the bowler's arm for each day of the game. He was in the posh box, so I was on my own.

The Test now features as one of Michael Manley's 'Great West Indian Performances'. Australia were a decent side – their attack led by Lawson and Alderman had recently proved far too good for England. Here in Barbados, their batters made 429, with almost everyone contributing. Then West Indies replied with 509, local boy Desmond Haynes getting 145, Richie Richardson 131 and skipper Lloyd 76. Then another Barbadian, Malcolm Marshall, cleaned up in Australia's second innings, taking 5-42 off sixteen overs. Holding did the rest, and the West Indies won by ten wickets.

I don't remember this. I looked it up. But what I do remember is my fellow spectators. The Kensington Oval was packed, hot and above all noisy with drums, whistles, shouts and incredibly loud conversations shouted among the watchers. Every comment – some of which passed me by – would be met with peals of laughter. Just in front of me was a group of about half a dozen large black guys, a couple of whom were enormously fat. As soon as play started, they brought out a crate of Banks beer, which they drank at an alarming rate. Their numbers seemed to change and grow, but still they kept hammering away at the beers. By the afternoon, the whole two front rows were shin-deep in empty bottles. It turned out that they were the recently crowned 'Banks Champion Beer Drinkers' of the island, and these tickets, and the everlasting supply of beer, were their prize.

When the West Indian quicks were bowling, this group became the nexus of the excitement of everyone in the nearby seats. The volume of noise went up and up, the jokes became even more unsuitable for my thirteen-year-old ears, and the shouts of support ever more bloodthirsty: 'Knock 'im head off!; 'Ribs! Ribs! Hit 'im in de heart.' Wow, so cool! Forget stuffy, desiccated Lord's – this was more like it. How could the same game that had bored me to death in England be so different out here? I returned home buzzing, wide-eyed, exhausted, and completely converted to cricket.

Of course, it was much too late for me to be any good. But a combination of enthusiasm and an uncoached and uncoordinated action that somehow produced inswing, saw me scrape into 'B' or 'C' teams at school. Once we had moved back to England, my dad, relenting in his opinion that I was completely hopeless, started coming to watch me play. He, like me, had become gripped by Caribbean history and its cricket. We both enjoyed and marvelled at the exploits of the West Indian team.

What an awesome team, or succession of teams, the Windies sent out! Between 1976 and 1991 they won eighteen of their twenty-two Test match series. In the seven Test series against England in the same period they won twenty-two matches and England just one.

It had started on the 1975 tour to Australia. Lillee and Thomson were at their most ferocious, and the West Indians were humiliated. Biased umpiring and racist abuse from Australian crowds deepened the misery. From now on, decided the new captain Clive Lloyd, it would be different. The fitness levels for the whole team were revolutionised, and the fastest bowlers were found, nurtured and unleashed. Combining this with brilliant batters, and superbly disciplined and skilful fielding, the West Indies became the kings of cricket.

The team's success lit up the Caribbean. The smaller islands in particular, historical anomalies all, were struggling to survive in a world of global economies of scale. They felt small, adrift and poor. People were leaving if they could. But, as Tony Cozier could proudly boast: 'We are not underdeveloped or third world in cricket.' 'Several dots on the map dominating the world?!' exclaims fast bowler Andy Roberts in *Fire in Babylon*. 'It was joy beyond words!' 'My bat was my sword,' wrote Viv Richards. 'I would like to think I carried my bat for the liberation of Africa and other oppressed people everywhere.'

****

West Indies cricket has suffered a vertiginous decline in the years since. Some put this down to a fading of British influence in the islands, as US television beams its own sports over the region. Others see football sweeping all before it. Whatever the reasons, after all the proud claims for cricket made by Lloyd, Richards et al., this slump is a hard blow, perhaps demonstrating the folly of tying your flag (in the case of the West Indies, a specially invented one) to the mast of sporting success. Unlike in real life, power and pre-eminence in cricket has so far always shifted, albeit usually slowly. No one stays at the top for ever; whether the West Indies will rule again is more uncertain. I hope they do.

****

Tea is finishing up. Some of the opposition's Asian contingent have held brief prayers, their mats pointed towards the impressive bulk of Canary Wharf, almost merging with the grey sky to the south-east. Around us three or four other games are underway, mostly kids, and almost all Asian or black. They are loud and enthusiastic. Meanwhile, our openers, Sam and Will, start slowly. The bowling is tight. After only a handful of overs, the rain that has been threatening all afternoon arrives, a light drizzle at first. We press on, with the ball getting soaked and the pitch slippery. There is no dampening of the noise made by the opposition, which makes our efforts look rather anaemic. I'm busy chasing wrappers from the tea now blowing across the grass and trying to keep warm. Seeking to up the tempo, our batters take a quick single. But Will slips, falls to the ground short of the crease and is run out. He's halfway to the boundary when he realises that the opposition is calling him back, in what Tony later describes as 'a spontaneous act of decency'. But he is out soon after his return to the crease, and by now the rain is getting heavier. On the boundary, we pack up bags and put on all the clothes we can find. The wind picks up, delivering the icy rain at an angle perfect for penetrating the tiny gap between pulled-down hat and upturned collar and trickling down to chill the spine. Someone puts up my umbrella, and it is instantly whipped inside out and wrecked. It's getting difficult to score as the paper is soaked and it's hard to see what's going on through the rain.

At last, enough is enough. It's a bloody storm out there. The final straw is that Jon Hotten, now batting, is wearing glasses, and he can't see a thing. With a frantic dash, everyone's off the pitch looking for shelter. After a bit of rushing around, the Authors end up under the eaves of the 'pavilion', and the ELCCC huddle under a cherry tree about a hundred yards away. We're soaked and freezing cold, and a few of our number start making noises about their long journey home. After a brief discussion, Charlie and I run over to the tree to consult with the opposition. Perhaps rather insensitively, I suggest we all decamp to the pub; their one white player is keen and starts suggesting options. The others move away, pretending they haven't heard. Anyway, they're hoping to restart as soon as the rain lessens a bit.

When, after half an hour or so, this at last happens, we agree to a new target from a reduced number of overs. Luckily for us, Sam is still in and, supported by Jon, he gets into his stride. This guy can really play, and sees us home with a few balls to spare, helped perhaps a little by the fact that the opposition use no fewer than nine different bowlers. So in theory we are the victors, though we all know that the new target was generous and without the rain we may well have lost. We agree to mark it down – our first ever Authors XI match – as a rain-affected draw.

Not that this really matters to any of us. Through the shared hardship of the wind and rain, and our shared love of cricket, we have bonded as a team, and with the opposition. From some of our lot there are mutterings about the artificial pitch, the atrocious outfield and lack of sight-screens, but in spite of these few grumbles the fixture is an undoubted success, much to my relief, with all of the Authors XI won over by the charm, enthusiasm, humour and old-fashioned sportsmanship of the ELCCC.

Our team was divided into those who felt our first match was a victory, and those who saw it as a fine bit of negotiation by our youngest player, Amol – who showed himself to be a formidable operator both on and off the field. He took our first wicket with a wide and he suggested the total that we should chase. Even now I can't quite decide whether we would have gone on to win if the rain hadn't come down. But with Sam at the crease, we felt that anything was possible.

Our next fixture was the first in back-to-back matches, putting a strain on our creaking bodies. But in each game, we faced players in their seventies, who showed us how the game should and could be played. First up, the Heartaches, down at James Holland's idyllic ground in Chalke Valley.

FIELD OF DREAMS
James Holland

Authors XI vs the Heartaches CC, 19 May, Chalke Valley

If you build it, he will come.

Field of Dreams

I t is the third week of May, my favourite month. In the Chalke Valley, in my little corner of south-west Wiltshire, I am awoken every morning by a cacophony of birdsong. The hedgerows are bursting with green, while the horse chestnuts drip with dark, fecund leaves and startling blossom. The days have dramatically lengthened, the evenings fresh with expectancy and hope. Lawnmowers buzz, cut grass richly scented on the air. Summer is here.

Most importantly, the cricket season is here, the long winter of purgatory over at last. Of course, I have been in the nets during the winter, and the first match has been a month earlier, but the bareness of the trees in April and the chill wind whistling down the valley has meant it is only now that it really feels as though everything is in place, that the landscape has plumped out with the rich rotundity of summer.

And what a week of cricket it promises to be: coaching the club's juniors on Monday, a T20 League match on Tuesday, Lord's for the Test match on Thursday, a net with my brother on Friday and then my first match for the Authors here at our new Chalke Valley ground on Saturday. Cricket, cricket, cricket. I can think of little else. Not even as a teenager watching Ian Botham was I as obsessed as I am now.

A lot of this is down to the New Ground, a project that has taken up much energy and many hours over the past few years. Isn't it every cricket lover's dream to build a new ground of one's own? In truth, it is not mine at all, but the Chalke Valley Cricket Club's, but I can't help feeling more than a little bit proprietorial.

During the winter, I tend to walk up there every week, taking my dog, and ambling on to the towering chalk downs of Marleycombe Hill, beneath which the ground nestles, and along the top of the ridge, and down again, past the ash trees with their gaggle of croaking rooks, and back around the northern, village, edge of the cricket field. In the beginning, there was just the field: lying there, waiting to become a cricket ground. Then half the field was fenced off, seven acres that would become the ground; then it was harrowed; soon after that, the square was dug out and vast amounts of loam poured in, a patch of ochre amidst the deeper brown soil around it. Finally, around early July of that incredible first summer of its embryonic life, a light sheen of green appeared. By September, it was grass – dense grass, one type and colour for the outfield, another, lusher, for the square. By walking up on to Marleycombe every week, it was possible to see the dream grow and develop, bit by bit. I even took to taking a photograph from the same spot each time. By the following spring, it really was a cricket field. Sight-screens had arrived, and even a temporary tented pavilion. I have never tired of this walk.

The week of cricket has begun well. Nearly thirty children careering around the ground on Monday evening, some in nets, others doing fielding drills that are way more interesting and fun than they ever were when I was younger, while the smaller ones play a softball game with blue plastic bats. On Tuesday, a match against the New Inn, and, incredibly, they have Glenn Maxwell playing for them – Aussie star of the Big Bash and scorer of the fastest fifty ever in Australia. He's over playing league cricket for South Wilts and then due to join Hampshire. Somehow, someone has coerced him into playing for a pub side. He smacks fifty in no time, facing one ball more than he did in Australia – a credit of sorts to the Chalke Valley bowling attack. Then he retires, a big grin on his face. Even more incredibly, Chalke Valley go on to win, smug faces all round as the players swig post-match cans of lager and cider.

Now it's Wednesday, and, with no cricket to play but with the sun shining, I decide to take another stroll up Marleycombe, and to have a look at the strip Ian, our groundsman, is preparing for Saturday's Authors match. It's a stiff climb to the top, but good exercise – think of those quick singles, I tell myself. In any case, the view from up there is always worth it, and on this sunny afternoon in May, three years on from when the first seed was sown, it looks perfect: the square striped with uncannily straight lines, the white of the pavilion and sight-screens almost dazzling against the rich green of the grass. And, yes, there is Saturday's strip, now protected with our latest acquisition: a set of covers.

I sit down on an old and soft anthill and think how permanent the ground now looks and then my thoughts return to that autumn four and a half years earlier. On the far side of the ground, behind a cedar and some beech trees, lies the village church, its tower just visible. Beyond that is Church Field, and in that first Saturday in November I was helping a friend set up the village fireworks display. During a pause I had ambled off and, climbing a fence, realised I was standing in what had once, years before, been Bowerchalke's cricket ground. Walking on a little further, I saw two partly covered rectangles of concrete – the old nets. At one end of the field stood a row of rusty-leaved horse chestnuts; at another, a terrace of brick and flint farmworkers' cottages. Ahead, beyond, Marleycombe rose up, sentinel over centuries of village life.

The field was nothing but rough grass now, home to two dozen Friesians. But once, Bowerchalke had been a great side. Through the sixties and early seventies, they were one of the most successful clubs around, sustained by the Gulliver clan, a family of fine cricketers. But then, when the Gullivers had been spotted and encouraged to play for Wiltshire, the decline had been swift. Within a couple of years the club had collapsed, the square handed back to the dairy herd, the cricket ground gone, it seemed, for ever.

Bowerchalke's decline was Broad Chalke's gain. A couple of miles closer to Salisbury, it was at Broad Chalke, where I had been born and brought up, that I had cut my cricketing teeth. My father came from a family of superb cyclists; he had always followed football and Aston Villa in particular, and had become a fine golfer, too. Cricket, however, had not been one of his childhood sports. Nonetheless, a couple of years after arriving in Broad Chalke (in 1970, when I was born), he had been asked to turn out for the village cricket team. They were one short: would he make up the numbers? It had been a Damascene moment for him, and for the next two decades he barely missed a game. Family holidays had to be taken in September after the league season was over. My mother somehow put up with him playing every Saturday and Sunday all summer.

Curiously, despite his prowess in other sports, he never excelled at his new passion. For twenty-five years he batted mostly at eleven and only later in his career – with a highlight of 7-23 – did he bowl for the 2nd XI. His top score ever with the bat was twenty-one. This lack of a starring role never put him off one iota. Quite the reverse. Mornings of home matches were often spent helping to prepare the wicket, marking out the boundary with a squeaky wheeled line marker, and sweeping up the fag butts from the pavilion.

The smell of that old wooden shack of a pavilion is still vividly clear to me: dust, stale tobacco and whitewash. There was a hatch for the scorers, and two seats made up from old wooden crates and leather car seats. A curtain on a rail divided the two teams. Throughout the seventies, there was no loo for the wives but a rough urinal for the men: a curved strip of corrugated iron into which they could drain their pre-match pints. I used to follow my father down to the pavilion, help him sweep and trim the grass around it, then later follow him down to the ground, watching the players change while anxiously waiting for the match to begin. Dave Hewitt, straggly haired, bearded, a big, hairy gut hanging over his Y-fronts, fag in one hand. He was the 'keeper. Trevor Summerell, looking the spit of the Australian opener, Graham Yallop. Trevor opened, too. There was Tim Barter, the captain – a dashing bat, also bearded, but with a gentle, easy charm. I always rather looked up to him. And there was Bob Dixon, who had a pair of pads that had once belonged to 'I. T. Botham'. It wasn't just my father who played week in week out; they all did. The same bunch, save a few who went missing every harvest time, playing every match, every year, for what seemed like for ever. It was a way of life, and I was utterly seduced by it, every bit as much as my father had been. I began playing at school, and then we even built a net at home. There wasn't much of a run-up, and what there was went uphill, but neither I nor my brother, nor our father for that matter, cared about that. As soon as the Easter holidays came around, up went the nets. The season had begun once more.

My brother, Tom, left home, went to university and then to London. I took a bit longer to leave the valley, but eventually ended up in London, too, and when I married we even lived just around the corner from Tom and his wife, Sadie. But Brixton was not the Chalke Valley. I missed home. I missed the chalk landscape, the spire of Salisbury's delicate cathedral. I missed the space, the freedom from traffic. I missed the cricket. Playing on recreational grounds somewhere in south London wasn't the same.

I'll be honest. I never had a burning childhood passion to become either a writer or a historian. I liked writing, and I was always interested in history, but it was not until my late twenties that it occurred to me that I might be able to make a living out of both. But what freedom it would offer: an escape from the city, a return to Wiltshire. A return to the Chalke Valley. Writers could live wherever they liked. I started on a novel with a backdrop of the Battle of Britain, allowed my obsessive nature to take hold and then managed to sell a work of history about Malta in the Second World War. The advance was enough to allow me to take the plunge, give up the day job and move back to the country. Well, not just the country. To Broad Chalke.

There were many familiar faces and much that had changed little in the ten years I'd been gone. The one big exception was the cricket club. Broad Chalke was no longer called Broad Chalke CC, but Chalke Valley CC. The old ground was now 'Chalke Valley Sports Centre', the recipient of a major lottery grant, but for the whole valley of six villages, hence the change to a more inclusive name. The old wooden shed had gone, replaced by a breeze-block and metal club house. Beside it, encroaching on to the outfield, was a brand new all-weather and walled tennis court. Another part of the outfield had been eaten into with a car park of rough scalpings. The charm of the old ground, now much reduced in size, had gone. So, too, had Dave Hewitt, Tim Barter et al. Even my father had finally hung up his boots. The cricket club was barely functioning – half a dozen friendly matches played on Sundays and that was it. Those running it were retired cricket lovers who rarely played themselves, but were desperate to keep it going. The square was spongy and erratic, the outfield plagued with clover and buttercups. Even worse, no one bothered to mark out the boundary any more. The squeaky old line marker had gone. White plastic triangles were pushed into the ground and that was it.

It was heartbreaking. Over the next few years, however, the Club managed to get back on track. A few more players, a T20 mid-week league, more matches. Even a new line marker. A grant provided us with sight-screens; a fundraiser, some loam for the square. Two of us went off and did coaching courses and we started a junior section. Things were looking up for Chalke Valley Cricket Club, but hovering over us was an unavoidable problem: the ground was shrinking. A new village school had been built right next to it; a skate park had further eaten into our outfield. The football club had been promoted and needed a larger pitch, which now nudged the square. A cricket ball narrowly avoided hitting a tennis player; another big six missed a moving car by inches. The field had originally been given to the cricket club back in 1958, but there was no longer room for cricket at the Chalke Valley Sports Centre.

As I stood there on the old Bowerchalke ground that bright early November afternoon, I almost heard the voices whispering through the leaves. *Build it and they will come.* I closed my eyes a moment. The sweet sound of ball on bat, a bowler's appeal, a ripple of applause. *Yes*, I thought, *of course.* This was the answer. We were *Chalke Valley* Cricket Club now. We could play anywhere in the valley, no longer bound to Broad Chalke. It would be sad to leave, but tragic to let the club fold. We could, I thought, play *here*. Breathe new life into the old ground: a field on which cricket, and cricket only, would be played. A ground of rare beauty. We would never be short of players – after all, who wouldn't want to play in such lovely surroundings? I wandered back, heart racing, gripped by an overexcited sense of certainty that I had unlocked the key to the club's future.

The first hurdle was convincing the core members of the club. Most Englishmen don't like change and are cautious and conservative by nature, and especially those in south-west Wiltshire. Yet to my surprise and delight, they were, to a man, all for it. We all went to the old Bowerchalke ground, walking over the field, fuelling our excitement. But there was caution, too. How much would we need to build a new cricket field? Where would we get it from? Grants, I said airily. Public subscription. Fundraisers. 'I don't know yet, but if we want it to happen, we can make it happen. I know we can.'

But then came disappointment. The farmer did not want the field being turned back into a cricket ground; it had just been awarded a hard-fought-for Higher Level Stewardship and he could not break the contract. This was a blow. Standing there a few weeks earlier I had been utterly convinced that this was where the cricket club's future lay. I'd heard those voices on the air urging me to build it. Could I really have been wrong? No, I could not. There *had* to be a new ground, here in Bowerchalke. I would not let this drop. I asked another farmer, but, despite some early enthusiasm, he could not find a field he was prepared to rent to us. Another agreed, but the area she had in mind was too small. Weeks passed, then months. Suddenly, it was March and while walking over Marleycombe I looked down and saw the ideal spot. The steep chalk slopes dropped down to a line of trees, but beyond, stretching some three hundred yards towards the churchyard, was a long and largely flat rectangular field. It was perfect: tucked away and out of sight of any road or telegraph pole, and overlooked by the soft but majestic curve of Marleycombe. The old ground was very pretty, but this field would make a stunning cricket field. With the same mounting excitement I had felt the previous November, I hurried to Caroline

Rawle's house, the other side of the churchyard. Caroline was a widow, her husband a former bomber pilot during the war, and then later a farmer. She was also a pillar of the community. I wondered why I'd not thought of her before, but now here I was, knocking on her door and conscious that she was probably our last chance. The door opened and she ushered me in. Rather breathlessly, I explained the situation and our desire for a brand new ground.

'Come on,' she said, 'let's have a look now.'

Caroline loved cricket and she wanted to do what she could to breathe more life into the village. This particular field – Butts Field – was hers, she explained, rather than the farm's. As we crossed her garden and out on to the path that lined the village end of the field, she wondered whether perhaps half of it would be enough. About seven acres. Maybe seven and a half. More than enough. That was the same size of land Thomas Lord had bought for his original ground north of the Marylebone Road back in 1786.

'So does this mean yes?' I asked.

'Yes,' she smiled. 'I can't think of anything more exciting.'

A hallelujah moment. We had our field. I hadn't been imagining those voices after all.

****

It's Thursday and I'm at Lord's, where England are playing the West Indies. It's a bit overcast but dry enough, and I've arrived at the ground before my friend Bill. I like getting there early to watch the players practising and as I amble under the media centre there is a hold-up as several players walk off the Nursery Ground. There's Alastair Cook and then Kevin Pietersen. He's not everyone's cup of tea, but I've been avidly following him with childish devotion since 2005. It was a hot July day and my brother and I were walking part of Offa's Dyke. England were playing Australia

in a pre-Test one-day international. As we crossed the River Wye
towards Hay with some eighteen miles' yomping under our belts,
Tom said, 'Wouldn't it be great if there was a pub around the first
corner we come to, showing the cricket and we watch England
smash Australia?'

And there was, and they did. It was one of the best three hours
of watching cricket I can remember and KP scored ninety-odd.
We both became acolytes on the spot. Nearly seven years on, here
he is standing right in front of me, and although collecting
autographs is supposed to be the preserve of teenage boys (I had
Ian Botham's fourteen times over), I thrust my ticket and a pen in
front of him and he duly signs it and actually says, 'Thanks.' *Will
he come?* I wonder.

Build it and they will come. Who exactly? More club members?
That was certainly true, just as I had hoped. We had more qualified
coaches, more junior members and more senior members, too.
Glenn Maxwell had come. So, too, had David English and his
team of Bunburies: Jeff Thomson, Graeme Hick, Peter Trego from
Somerset, James Brooks from Northants, among a host of sporting
heroes. That had marked our Grand Opening, a wonderful day of
burning blue skies, blazing sun and cricket, and even a Spitfire
twirling overhead. And, coincidentally, my fortieth birthday; it's
not my fault my birthday is in June. It was, of course, the best
birthday I had ever had. Being chirped at by Graeme Hick as I
opened the innings for Chalke Valley; chewing the cud over a pint
with Thommo. Catching out Peter Trego. 'You're living the
dream,' said Rachel, my wife, as she produced a cricket bat
birthday cake at tea. Too right.

I find my seat in the Upper Compton Stand and look out over
Lord's, the stately pavilion at the far end, the ground as immaculate
as ever. I wonder if our new ground will last as long as Thomas
Lord's has done. Our lease is for ninety-nine years, our rent a
philanthropic peppercorn a year, which we paid in advance in a

silver pepperpot presented to Caroline Rawle, our new President, on our Grand Opening day.

The current Lord's was not built in a day, although it took Thomas Lord a year to get his rough patch of grassland as flat as a bowling green. The first match had also been played in June, back in 1814. It took us much the same amount of time, although only after a year of preparation and feverish fundraising to get to a position where there was enough in the pot to start work. A 'New Ground Committee' had been formed, consultations with the villagers made, planning permission sought, access issues slowly resolved, and the laborious process of fundraising begun. Endless grant forms were filled in, begging letters sent out to the great and the good of the entire valley and beyond. Another committee was formed to plan and prepare for the Grand Opening day, which was hoped would prove another big fundraiser. It was an all-consuming process, two steps forward one step back, but that movement forward always provided more than enough of a spur.

By the end of 2010, we had raised more than £85,000. My original vision had been of a rough field, with a wooden shack for a pavilion, just as Broad Chalke's ground had been in the seventies. Ambitions had risen quickly, however. 'If we're going to do this,' said Peter Walker, our new chairman, 'then I think we should do it properly.' Hear, hear, I replied, visions of building the finest cricket ground since the creation of the Rose Bowl. The outfield was harrowed and 'buryvated' – in which a machine collected any pebble or stone and buried it six inches into the soil. One hundred and forty-five tons of Kayloam from Oxford was set into the nine-inch-deep dug-out square. Two permanent 'non-turf' wickets (as they are officially termed) were laid, one at the edge of the square, another on a second, training pitch, rather like the Nursery Ground at Lord's. New mowers and scarifiers were bought and a set of gang mowers. Ian Newman, a man who had been born in

Bowerchalke and who has lived in the valley much of his life, offered his services. 'If there's anything I can do,' he said, 'anything at all, let me know.'

'Could you help with maintaining the ground?'

Yes, he said, he'd love to. We sent him on a groundsman's course and he now goes to bed every night with a book about groundsmanship beside him. Ian is at the ground every day; I am not the only member of our club with an obsessive nature.

The magnificent pavilion facing me now at the far end of Lord's was not built until 1890, some seventy-five years after the first match was played at the ground. In the Chalke Valley, we had to accept that our pavilion, however modest, might take a little time to build, too. We had bought a temporary pavilion via the Rose Bowl. When the Hampshire ground had undergone redevelopment, there were two hospitality tents that were sold off and we bought one of them. It is very white, with a twin-peaked roof and metal sides – hardly a tent at all. Two internal walls were added to create a set of changing rooms, and electricity connected. It has good provenance and has served us well.

A permanent wooden pavilion remains part of the vision, however. A clock in the roof, with a long verandah, and a club room with a bar and old team photos – simple, but complying with new ECB and government building regulations. An old piece of folded corrugated iron will no longer do, nor a dividing curtain to hide the blushes of those changing. A new pavilion, no matter how traditional in appearance, now requires disabled access, thirteen – not eleven – seats, two showers and a loo per changing room, and a female and disabled loo as well. These loos also require their own sewage system. The old Broad Chalke pavilion looked as though it was put up by a work party over a couple of weekends, at a cost of twenty pounds, but our planned new pavilion looks set to cost closer to fifty thousand. It is a lot of money.

Half that money, however, now sits tantalisingly on the table, a grant offered by the Foundation of Sports and Arts. All we have to do is match it, and the sum is ours, and our pavilion, the final piece of the new ground, will be complete. Chair of that foundation, and the person who has played a key part in securing the grant, is none other than Tim Rice, lyricist, Oscar winner and cricket lover, and it is he who is arriving at our new ground on Saturday with his team of Heartaches to play the Authors.

****

A good day at Lord's, with England's bowlers on top, but then it is back home and a net with my brother, who has come down a day early for Saturday's game. He's depressed because he feels he's not bowling well. Actually, he's rather good – he has a nice, easy action and gets both seam movement and away swing, and now seems to have a bit of extra nip, too. I find myself playing and missing at a few and tell him I think he's bowling as well as I've ever seen him. I mean it, too, although I'm not sure he's convinced. I have no such feelings of self-doubt. The previous summer I was struggling to get many runs. I wasn't doing anything differently, but simply kept getting out. Was this it, I had wondered? Was I entering middle-age decline? 'I feel so depressed about it,' I told Rachel. 'It's ruining my summer and my life.'

'Well, in that case you'd better give up,' she replied with a startling lack of sympathy.

Unfortunately for Rachel, the doubts of the previous summer have gone. This year, for some inexplicable reason, I'm seeing the ball better, hitting the ball better, and feeling in decent touch. Confidence has returned.

When Saturday dawns, and with the sun out and clear skies, I am, however, conscious of a gnawing nervousness. I feel like a proud father showing off his baby. The Authors have not been to Chalke Valley's ground before and nor has our leading benefactor,

Tim Rice. I worry that I have oversold it, and feel suddenly self-conscious about the portable loo out at the back of the temporary pavilion and the lack of showers. We are no longer living in the seventies; cricket teams expect decent facilities.

I needn't have worried. Most of both the Authors and the Heartaches have come from London and, despite the trek down, they say all the right things, and I find myself beaming proudly. And despite the underdeveloped plumbing, the ground does look very fine indeed. The boundary is marked by 400 metres of thick rope. A large black score box waits ready, while around the edge of the outfield is an array of chairs and benches. The new covers stand idle and pristine at one side. The square is perfectly striped, while the wicket itself looks bleached and rock hard. There are no more spongy puddings to play on here. Beyond, the chalk downs of Marleycombe rise over us, gentle and avuncular.

The game is a close one. We bat first and score 186-7. Sam Carter scores another effortless fifty, although I am not in the runs myself – a slightly dubious caught behind. Most chip in, though, a twenty here, a seventeen there. Nonetheless, the total seems slightly under par, because, now that the club has covers, even in May it's a lovely strip to bat on.

Our own bowling is a little loose, and worryingly so, although, much to my great relief, my brother bowls tidily enough. But wickets do start to fall and suddenly our total looks safe after all. By the game's end, the Heartaches are twenty-three short for six wickets down. An honourable draw, then.

Afterwards, with the ground bathed in golden early summer light, we head to the pub where Sir Tim urges me to find the corresponding twenty-five grand for the pavilion. 'You've got to find it,' he says. 'Somehow, some way.' I know he's right. We will fill out more grant forms, hold more pub quizzes, plead and beg, and sell the Rose Bowl twin peaks. We can do it. Next year, when the Authors play, it will be there. *Build it and they will come* – generations of future cricketers playing at this field of dreams.

The result against the Heartaches had been a fair one and promised much for next season's fixture. Our next opponents were the Bushmen – a wandering side not unlike ours, with history behind them and a profession in common. I'd netted with them earlier in the season and had been impressed by the mixture of youthful vigour and experience. Jon, our Old Batsman, was positively youthful compared to some of their line-up.

CRICKET AND BROADCASTING
Jon Hotten

Authors XI vs the Bushmen CC,
20 May, Trevor Bailey Sports Ground, Dulwich

And after Trevor Bailey, it will be Christopher Martin-Jenkins.
John Arlott

L ast autumn, at the bottom of some boxes in the cellar of a
junk shop, I found John Arlott's book *Jack Hobbs: Profile of
the Master.* It was 10p. It began not in the modern way
with a boozy tour anecdote or a moment of tabloid controversy,
but with a poem that Arlott wrote in 1952, 'To John Berry Hobbs
on his Seventieth Birthday'. The first verse is:

There falls across this one December day
The light, remembered from those suns of June
That you reflected, in the summer play
Of perfect strokes across the afternoon.

Cricket is a game that exists in the mind; it is mostly played there.
Or, as the great Yogi Berra once said of something else: 'It is 90 per
cent mental. The other half is physical.' Its psychology is what

gives cricket a depth and dimension that has endured since it began, and as such it needs a language to describe it, to frame it, to convey adequately just what the hell it does to you. Most cricketers, at our level at least, spend far more time thinking about the game than playing, and a lifetime's experience of it is shaped by that.

****

'Nine runs off the over, twenty-eight Boycott, fifteen Gower, sixty-nine for two. And after Trevor Bailey, it will be Christopher Martin-Jenkins.' Those were the final words that John Arlott spoke into a radio microphone. It was 2 September 1980 at Lord's, the Centenary Test between England and Australia. The PA man announced that Arlott had concluded his last piece of commentary and the crowd rose in a standing ovation. The Australian fielders lined up and in a rare concession to something other than his own innings, Boycott removed his batting gloves to applaud (Arlott once said of him, 'he had a lonely career'). John Arlott was sixty-six years old.

Four years later and a year after his own retirement from the game, Mike Brearley travelled to Arlott's home on Alderney to interview him for the BBC. It took a sentence for Arlott to get to the heart of the matter, to the centre of his life. Brearley began by asking him why he had chosen Alderney. 'Well,' said Arlott in a voice rising up over the hot coals in his chest, 'the tempo here is magnificent.' Not for him a description of the views or of the peace and quiet, but instead that connection he felt to the cadences of the place.

That was present in everything Arlott did, in the rhythm of his sentences, both spoken and written; the melancholic beats of his verse, the rise and fall of his commentary. The way that he could almost conduct a passage of Test cricket was his true talent as a speaker – 'in through the eyes, out through the mouth' as he used to put it – his internal sense of the rhythm of the over, and the session, and of the day and the match, all building symphonically. He confessed at one point that his favourite moments in Test matches were batting collapses, and again noted the way they produced their own momentum, fed by the noise of the crowd.

Not saying anything helped to produce that rhythm, too. When he spoke to Brearley about his parents, or about the son he lost in a car accident, he paused for long periods and the camera held his face, which bore all the iniquities of age. Its stillness, which he struggled to maintain, conveyed everything that words could not. 'No ...' he said eventually. 'Let's talk about something else.'

****

Perhaps I have always felt tied to Arlott in some way. His voice was present not just on *Test Match Special* but on the BBC's John Player Sunday League television coverage, where, come certain blessed Sabbaths, Hampshire were on and my greatest hero, Barry Richards, would open the batting. The names Arlott, Richards and Hotten formed an unbreakable trinity, even if, admittedly, neither of the other two knew anything about it. Richards was Hampshire's recalcitrant star, a South African genius exiled by the sporting boycott; Arlott first saw cricket at May's Bounty, and the Bounty was for me, born in Hampshire and playing for Basingstoke, my home ground. Some of the real old townies whose families stretched back into local history called it The Folly, which is how it was known before James May, scion of a brewing dynasty, gave it to the club for cricket. It sloped from the Castlefield End towards the town, and I once faced a bowler called Applejack as he ran down the hill in the gathering dusk, a spell far quicker than anything I'd seen before. On the scoreboard side of the ground was a crumbling school wall, and from the far corner trees swept around the boundary towards the pavilion. Arlott used to sit on that far side to watch. The outfield had the gentle undulations that really old cricket grounds have. Hampshire played a couple of games a year there, and Barry Richards held its record one-day score, 123 against Glamorgan in 1974. Several famous things had happened. Andy Sandham made his 100th first-class hundred on the Bounty, and Andy Roberts, godfather of West Indian quicks, once bowled a legendary bouncer that put Colin Cowdrey in hospital. I watched Alvin Kallicharran hit six after six out of the ground and into the road at the Town End, and saw a guy called David Rock make his maiden first-class hundred. When Jeff Thomson, right at the end of his career, played a season for Middlesex bowling off about eight paces, I carried his bag up to the dressing room.

Above them all was Richards, a player so ineffably brilliant that it is no effort to see him, all these years later, in my mind's eye: tall, slightly splay-footed, collar turned up, cap pulled down over seventies hair, teeth flashing through his tan. He stood stooped at the crease, feet almost together, but seemed to know where every ball was going before the bowler did. He made nine hundreds before lunch in his career, hit Dennis Lillee's Western Australia for 325 in a day on his own, got runs in a Durban club game by turning the bat around and using the edge, averaged seventy-two in the four Tests he did play.

Arlott said of Richards that he was 'a batsman of quite staggering talent', and I in turn cherished the only words that Barry Richards had ever spoken to me: 'I'm just eating my sandwich at the moment.' These were uttered as I sought his autograph during tea at a benefit game at Fleet CC, soon after he'd hit Dinger Bell, a local tearaway fast bowler, out of the ground, over the trees and on to the first green of the pitch and putt course.

****

The Trevor Bailey Sports Ground in Dulwich is not one of the world's greats. It's not one of Dulwich's greats, either, really, the faint charms of a line of oak trees counterpointed by the mottled tennis courts and their ragged nets next to the car park and in the field beyond the far end, the Ballardian spectre of an abandoned PA tower with a broken loudspeaker hanging from the top, suspended by a power cable. The ground bears Bailey's name because he played a lot of his early cricket in Dulwich before launching into a career so cussed that it generated not one but two nicknames in celebration, 'The Barnacle' and 'The Boil'.

All of this information flowed to me second-hand. For my generation, Bailey was most famous for *Test Match Special*, where he appeared with Fred Trueman as one of the expert summarisers, men who sat alongside the commentators and provided the earthy insight of the trenches – Trueman the autodidact philosopher king, regally dismissive of poetic flannel and southern nonsense; Bailey the flint-hearted pro with an unexpected aesthetic eye, and the man who had accompanied Arlott through that final spell. The divide between commentator and summariser was sometimes sharply etched: Henry Blofeld remembered how easily Bailey had slapped him into place early in his *TMS* career after Blofeld had said, hyperbolically by the standards of the mid-seventies, that Greg Chappell had just provided an unmatchable example of an off drive. 'Greg Chappell, of course,' sniffed Bailey, 'is better known for the on drive ...'

Trueman and Bailey got plenty of gentle ribbing back, Trueman for his tendency to rose-tint the past (especially any aspect of it that involved him), and Bailey for his legendary ability to remain at the crease almost runless for many hours at a time. Describing one particularly tenacious innings, Neville Cardus wrote: 'Before he gathered together 20 runs, a newly-married couple could have left Heathrow and arrived in Lisbon, there to enjoy a honeymoon. By the time Bailey had congealed 50, this happily wedded pair could easily have settled down in a semi-detached house in Surbiton; and by the time his innings had gone to its close they conceivably might have been divorced.'

It was Bailey's kind of day, steel-grey and windblown, the deeper ground still solid from winter, the grass clumped and knotted in places and the topsoil that held it thawing as summer slowly came. It was a day for grit, not flair, a day of penance to the weather gods for better things ahead. Like the Authors, the Bushmen had history. They were named after Bush House, home of the World Service, but were actually formed at Bletchley Park in 1942. (Their first game was interrupted, in true BBC fashion, by someone running on the pitch to announce the fall of Tobruk. He was ushered away by an umpire who later became Director-General.) The Bushmen are run on principles in keeping with the era of their birth; 'Bushmenlike Deeds' are rewarded and winning is regarded with the suspicion of the genuine amateur, victory's arrival as much of a mystery as its frequent disappearances. Their official history, written by Maurice Latey, lies with his papers in the Bodleian Library, Oxford. Estimable men have taken the field for them, including Learie Constantine, Trevor McDonald and Laurence Gretton, who first played for the club at the age of eleven, and went on to take more than eight hundred wickets in their colours.

The men emerging from their changing room looked younger and sharper than that, producers, reporters, directors, men of day-to-day action ranged against the more naturally contemplative, laid back and frankly less mobile Authors. At the Bushmen's head was a player we could all look up to, Michael Cockerell, one of the country's leading political documentary makers, a man who had interviewed eight prime ministers and had once been married to Harold Macmillan's granddaughter, but who, far more impressively than all of that, was still a key all-rounder at the age of seventy-one.

****

In *It Never Rains*, his wry diary of a County season, Peter Roebuck wrote: 'The dressing room, the car and the field are private places' (rereading that sentence now, it's impossible not to think of Sachin Tendulkar driving his Porsche on empty Mumbai freeways at 4 a.m., as he apparently does to finally feel alone). Professional players have always used their own language to describe the game, separate from how it was written about or commentated upon. It sometimes filtered down into club cricket, and, when it did, it felt like privileged information, entry into another room in which the game was played with mordant humour by men who made their living by surviving in it. Roebuck's book, which recounted Somerset's term of 1983, was a blade of light from the window of that room, illuminating an unseen corner. It was the first book I'd read that was equivocal about the game, that made it okay to feel ambiguous about something that dominated your life. It was self-aware, knowing, courageous in its way. Roebuck found cricket and his efforts at playing it funny, ridiculous, poignant, hubristic, bathetic in the sense that it switched from the everyday to the unrepeatable, and slightly, darkly heroic, too.

The start of his season is beset by rain, endless and total, that sends him indoors for hours and hours on the bowling machine. Roebuck's confidence grows and grows until he strides out for his first innings of the year and lasts one ball. As the summer reaches its height, he's in the grip of a six-week depression that concludes on the first day of August with the simple words 'no entry'. It's a book full of such cadences, the rhythms of real life that Arlott would have recognised and translated, too.

Then there are the identikit ring roads and the fuming pub grub, the grinding tyranny of the fixture list, the recognition of unfathomable talent far out of reach (Botham, Richards and Garner are perched in their corners of the Somerset dressing room), and the comforting quirkiness of any team, anywhere. What hits home the most, though, is the passage where Roebuck hears that he might be considered for England, and realises, deep down in his heart, that he doesn't really want to be, or at least that he is profoundly uncertain about it. That admission, and his honesty in revealing it, rounded the game out for me, completed it in my head. This was why it was great – because it was not easy. Somehow, the joy of it was increased by this. Whether you played cricket, wrote about it, thought about it, lived it or watched the odd highlights programme when there was nothing else on, you could never exhaust it. It was, and always would be, too rich, too human and complex, for that.

After Roebuck retired, he became a broadcaster and he had a rock-solid intellectual confidence that quite often set him at odds with prevailing opinion. But as his generation of pros disgorged many of their number into the commentary boxes of the world, they brought with them the language of the professional dressing room that he had begun to use in his book. As they did, everyone who watched and listened was soon familiar with it; the pitch that would rag, the swinging ball that hoops round corners, the jaffa that knocks over the dollies and so on. The distinction that had existed between a commentator, employed because he could describe the game, and the ex-pro who could analyse it, was over.

****

John Arlott once described John Easter as 'the slowest fast bowler in cricket', but then Arlott hadn't seen Michael Cockerell in his later years. There was something magnificent about Cockerell's tempo, and his endurance. He came in to bowl from a run that had at one time helped him to generate pace, but that was now an exercise in rhythm alone, his bowling arm still raised high in his delivery stride, wrist cocking well above the level of his head. It was an action grooved by the years, full of the echoes of what once was. From mid-innings until the winning runs were scrambled he must have bowled fourteen or fifteen overs off the reel, most landing on the spot, and they were delivered with a fast bowler's temperament, one that was probably useful in dealing with prime ministers, too, barking sharply at fielders who were out of position, demanding from the rest of the team as much as he asked of himself. Back on the bombshell pitches of the early era of the game, he might still have sent down the odd unplayable one, a George Hirst or Derek Shackleton, but the wicket at the Trevor Bailey Sports Ground was one that a man like Trevor Bailey would never have got out on, soft, slow, paceless and low.

Plenty of us had done, though. The Bushmen went in first. It was a timed game, meaning they would bat until they felt they'd set a fair chase with the time remaining. We fielded out there for forty-seven overs in the chilling spring. The distant pavilion glowed. I was wearing trainers following a pre-match incident with the sole of my boot. We didn't even get drinks, but then they would probably have been brought out by St Bernard. The Bushmen began slowly, contained in part by the dead pitch, by the dancing sprite at backward point that was William Fiennes, and by some solid bowling from Waheed, Nick and Charlie. By the time Cockerell walked in, they were five down for ninety and indebted for those to a well-struck fifty-eight from opener Nick Norman-Butler. Age may have robbed Cockerell of the muscle to send the ball moving quickly over the rough outfield, but when he was joined by Pianki Assegai, the team's youngest member, the pair began an entertaining double act between the wickets, Cockerell, as he would when he bowled, snapping orders and turning down singles – on one occasion, Assegai ran two while the great man remained in his ground, scowling. Together, somehow, they got the score up to 157.

****

Over the years, I have played cricket with several men who have admitted to silently commentating on themselves as they batted.

I've never done it during a match, but while playing air shots in the garden? Holding a new bat? Mentally replaying a decent knock? Oh yes, then I have jerked Lord's to its feet, silenced the SCG, heard Barry Richards call me the best player since – well, Barry Richards. It's probably a ubiquitous habit among cricketers, and yet it is something that Grace or Fry or even the young Bradman would never have done. They were not commentated upon, and so they weren't aware of the game existing in that way, mediated by technology. In that respect, commentary is more contemporary than the game. (The first piece of live cricket broadcast came in 1927, the year before Bradman's Test debut. The young Arlott commentated, quite brilliantly, on The Don's final Test innings, cricket's most significant duck, but *Test Match Special* did not begin until 1957.) Thus they probably thought about the game slightly differently, framed a different vocabulary to describe it to themselves and to others.

Cricket's lingua franca is subject to those forces; broadcasting has shaped the mental landscape of the game, and continues to. There is a gap between the experience of those who grew up listening to Arlott and Benaud and those subject to its modern stylings. Twenty20 cricket, first played in 2003, is its new colossus, and it has exerted its force on the language as well as the field of play. The Indian Premier League has Ravi Shastri screaming 'ARE YOU READY' at the crowd and the viewer from the coin toss; its commercial imperatives have turned sixes into DLF Maximums and wickets into Citi Moments Of Success. (Sitting here, I don't have to look these things up. After a few hours of exposure to them they are as deeply imprinted as Arlott's deathless description of Clive Lloyd cover driving in the 1975 World Cup final – 'the shot of a man knocking the top off a thistle with a walking stick'.) T20 has changed the language in other ways, too. It has introduced range hitting and relay fielding, slower-ball bouncers, and many other quirks of technique and invention.

There is barely a game of any note in any format that is not available to watch somewhere, on satellite TV or online, and that has changed the language, too. There can be few cricket fans unaware that 'doosra' is Urdu for 'other one', 'teesra' is 'Third One', that a 'zooter' was invented by Shane Warne, terms that have crept from the middle to the box and out into the wider world. For all of the gains in the richness and variety of the language, there have been losses, as the microphones have been almost wholly assumed by former professional cricketers.

Trevor Bailey was not expected to describe Botham, as Arlott unforgettably did, as 'coming in from the Kirkstall Lane End like a shire horse cresting the breeze', just as Arlott wasn't obliged to hold forth on facing Wes Hall. And yet men who have never seen the game in the way that Arlott or Brian Johnston have seen it are expected to describe it as well as analyse it, and with that something has gone. You must feel for the kids growing up with the inner voice of Nick Knight or Danny Morrison accompanying them.

****

What would the commentators make of the Authors? Well, they might have difficulty identifying them for a start. Anyone lingering over the soft-focus black and white images that adorn the jackets of the books written by these men would not have recognised the burst-sofa torsos and ageing faces picking through the floored kit of the dressing room, or taking the field with a creaking sprint or a desperate stretch. (Early in the season, the effects of Darren Maddy's Edgbaston callisthenics were still there to be seen: men rolling on the ground in strange, sometimes dangerous positions.) Some very recently published books evidently bore author photographs taken years, perhaps decades, previously, from a distance and in flattering sepia tones.

They might, though, recognise some archetypes, because there are many of those in cricket (and language plays a role in how you see yourself as a cricketer). Nick Hogg, for example, is a bearded, buccaneering Botham sort. He bowls swing, and once confessed to me while we were batting together that he found it difficult not to want to 'murder' every ball bowled to him. Richard Beard, with his natural introspection and the batsman's deep-rooted distrust of the game and what it might do to him, was a figure Boycott might identify with, especially as he compiled a careful, ultimately decisive forty-odd in the run chase against the Bushmen. Partnering him in a long stand was William Fiennes, a deeply elegant player who nonetheless in his on-field mannerisms and general demeanour bears a passing resemblance to Phil Tufnell. Tony McGowan, when required to field close to the bat, has a habit of removing his cap and thrusting it down his trousers as an impromptu box, a quirk that no doubt would have pleased Trueman. Amol Rajan is a cricketer who might have fascinated them, the sort who, were he a pro, would soak up column inches, who'd find himself on front pages as well as back; a Lamb, a Javed Miandad, a Warne. He wears odd pads when he bats, and a strange pair of white boxing boots. He seeks out confrontation, and, more than that, he creates some if he can't find any. Batting, bowling, fielding, he doesn't care. He's the type that commentators love because he will 'make something happen'. A quiet passage of play in the field, with the gentle lull of summer overs ticking by, will be interrupted with a deliberately provocative sledge. He's not bothered who it's with, either. Once in a game when keeping wicket, Will mistakenly shouted 'well fielded, Waheed' when Amol threw one in from cover.

'Yeah …Yeah … We all look the fucking same, don't we …' was his instant response.

Will, undoubtedly the nicest man in cricket, must have been flustered by this, because, a couple of overs later, he did it again.

As the rest of the field dissolved into helpless laughter, Amol bounced up and down on the balls of his feet, clapping his hands while Will cringed. Later in the same game, he picked a fight with a fast bowler who was twice his height, running down the wicket to him and laughing when he missed the ball.

****

Broadcasting has reshaped cricket in the new age in a way beyond words. On 24 November 2009, in the Test match between New Zealand and Pakistan at Dunedin, the Decision Review System was used for the first time. Each element of the DRS, the ball-tracking technology, hot-spot and snickometer, were technologies first developed by television for the benefit of viewers and commentators rather than players and umpires. Snicko first appeared on Channel 4 in 1999, Hawk-Eye on the same channel in 2001 and Hotspot on Sky in 2006, and, until they were integrated into the governance of cricket, television viewers knew things about the game that the players did not. It meant that the process of umpiring became more talked about and examined, and the biggest change came in the perception of lbw decisions: i.e. umpires began to give them once Hawk-Eye demonstrated the number of deliveries that were going on to hit the pegs.

'What were wrong wi' that one, were it going under t'stumps?' was one of Fred Trueman's famous grumbles to the men in white, a complaint he wheeled out periodically on *TMS* when days were wet and discussion turned to his mighty career. It won't be heard from Graeme Swann should he migrate to the commentary position. Of his first 193 Test match wickets, fifty-five have been lbw, or 29 per cent. Jim Laker, the great and stoic offie who went on to have many years muttering almost inaudibly into a microphone for BBC television, had thirty-two of his 193 that way, or 17 per cent. In 2004 Test spinners took 16 per cent of their wickets lbw; in 2012 it was 33 per cent. Of the five spinners with the highest percentage of wickets dismissed lbw in the history of the game, three are currently playing.

It's a beast that feeds itself, of course. Spinners bowl straighter because their chances are higher. The chances of a leg before in a club game have always been subject to more random forces, but the concept and the language have filtered downwards from the top. For a season or two, an amateur umpire making the television replay signal was guaranteed a sycophantic laugh from the field. Now, they are ready and willing to yield to a speculative appeal with the batsman some way down the wicket towards the bowler. (In fairness, 'twas occasionally ever thus. I recall many years ago being given out by the opposition umpire to one that wouldn't have hit another set of stumps. 'Sorry, mate,' a fielder said as I trooped off. 'He always does that.' 'Oh, does he,' I thought …)

The game with the Bushmen needed no technical intervention. A win for the Authors came from a scrambled single as a leaden afternoon transmuted almost invisibly into dusk. Through a gloom that would have had Dickie Bird considering not if play was possible, but whether it was his bedtime, we could just pick out Charlie diving in at the non-striker's end. Despite our best intentions, it wasn't really a day for lyricism, more suited to one of Trevor Bailey's *bons mots* than John Arlott's flights of fancy, but that was all right.

****

During Arlott's final years on Alderney, Ian Botham was one of his closest neighbours and friends. They had met, according to Botham, when he was a sixteen-year-old at Somerset and he was summoned to lug two of Arlott's hampers into the press box at Taunton. Arlott opened one, which was filled with wine, and asked Botham if he'd ever tried any. He proceeded to uncork several bottles and then open the other hamper, which contained cheeses chosen as accompaniments. Botham had met the man he still describes as his mentor.

As Arlott became increasingly ill, Botham would visit him every day. 'At the end when the emphysema took over and he was struggling with speech he had an oxygen mask and I often had to empty his bag for him,' Botham remembered. 'But he liked me being there because I knew to wait and let him finish his sentences between gasps. I didn't try to say the words for him because I knew how much they mattered.'

How much they did matter, and still do.

Arlott's obituary in *Wisden* called him 'a man of deep humanity'. Botham's words, and those in *Wisden*, would serve any man well as an epitaph, but on his headstone in the graveyard at St Anne's church are some of his own, from another of his poems: 'So clear you see those timeless things/That, like a bird, the vision sings'.

The vision sings. Thank you, John. Now, if Barry Richards would open with me, you know, just once, on the Bounty …

Our next game was the first of the two showpieces of the season (the other being our match at Lord's). The Authors XI were due to play the Lords and Commons CC at the breathtaking Wormsley ground on what turned out to be one of the best days of this rain-dominated summer. With the generous backing of our sponsors, Christie's, we'd decided to organise a charity fixture, in aid of First Story and Chance to Shine, and so we invited all and sundry to watch us play the politicians. But would people come? We might look the part, with our new shirts, but Wormsley crowds were used to watching current and former greats – from Brian Lara down. On the day, a crowd of several hundred turned up to watch one of the most fiercely contested matches of the season.

CRICKET AND THE ESTABLISHMENT
Amol Rajan

Authors XI vs Lords and Commons CC, 27 May, Wormsley

> *Cricket had plunged me into politics long before I was aware of it. When I did turn into politics I did not have too much to learn.*
>
> C. L. R. James, *Beyond a Boundary*

To no human endeavour has the witless platitude 'sport and politics don't mix' more often or erroneously been attached than cricket. My starting point here is the feeling that this cannot be mere coincidence. Taking politics out of cricket would be like taking the teacher out of a classroom; and the deeper one's love for the game, the more myopic and banal that phrase inevitably seems. Cricket is the most incorrigibly political of all sports, and it is precisely because it has always been the continuation of politics by other means that this silly mantra has so frequently been uttered by the tremulous faction within its ranks.

To understand why, we must look to its heritage. The history of cricket is a sequence of imperial inversions, in which the English are systematically defeated by those they have taught the game.

During the twentieth century, and particularly during that first half in which the flame of empire was still burning, the sport went from being a white man's blessing to a white man's burden, forever allowing natives to embarrass their colonial conquerors. In his seminal *Beyond a Boundary*, C. L. R. James explained how cricket galvanised anti-imperialism in the Caribbean. The Indian example is, perhaps, less well known.

In February 1927, Arthur Gilligan, a former captain of England, sat on the wicker chairs and close-trimmed lawns of Delhi's Roshanara Club. He was joined on that balmy evening by the Maharajah of Patiala, who had financed Gilligan's tour of India for MCC that winter, and the businessman Grant Govan and his Indian accomplice Anthony de Mello. Gilligan, perhaps curiously for a later member of the British Union of Fascists, had great affection for both his hosts and Indian civilisation generally. He went out of his way to urge the Indians to set up a board of control for cricket in India, adding that, if they did so, on his return to Lord's he would wield his considerable influence to argue that they should be admitted to the Imperial Cricket Conference (ICC). This he duly did. Two years later, as Mihir Bose notes in his fine book *A Maidan View*, India was a member of the ICC. Three years after that, it was playing Test cricket. A conversation at the Roshanara had led sport and politics to be suddenly out of sync: in politics, Indians were still subjects, an inferior race; in cricket, they were now equals. When the great Indian moderate leader Gopal Krishna Gokhale and his mentee, one Mohandas K. Gandhi, championed India's right to self-determination a few years later, they could cite cricket as evidence of an Indian's moral, intellectual and physical parity with their colonial masters. It may be an exaggeration to say that Arthur Gilligan and the MCC, rather than general imperial overstretch, world war or civil disobedience caused the end of the British Empire; but that they were an influence cannot be doubted. Sport and politics mix all right.

There are several other ways in which the imperial game generously lends itself to politics, too. First, in being originally a product of the English Establishment, and so bound up with the pretensions of aristocracy; second, in its unusual tendency to be a forum for heavy disputes between nations, as in the Bodyline series, the D'Oliveira affair and modern matches between India and Pakistan; and third, perhaps above all and most pertinently for this chapter, in the strategic cast of mind, cunning spirit and calculating disposition that it cultivates in all those who don the whites. The former two show that, more than with any other game, the raw materials of politics – empire, class, race and nationhood – are that of this sport also. The latter begins to explain the highly unusual tendency of its practitioners, once retired, to chase political glory.

Naturally other sports produce political careers, too. Non-playing executives can use sport as a springboard into politics. The Salt Lake City Olympics were the basis of Mitt Romney's successful bid for governor of Massachusetts. Silvio Berlusconi took AC Milan from corrupt under-performers to champions of Europe, and then launched his farcical political career by promising to 'make Italy like [AC] Milan', and naming his party Forza Italia, after a football chant. Mauricio Macri, a former chairman of Boca Juniors, became mayor of Buenos Aires. Mikhail Prokhorov, the lanky owner of the New Jersey Jets basketball team, failed to oust Vladimir Putin as Russian president. George W. Bush ran for Texas governor not as his father's son but as the former managing director of baseball side the Texas Rangers.

Actual players have gone into politics, too, of course. George Weah narrowly failed to win Liberia's presidential election in 2004. Eric Cantona launched a bid for the French presidency to draw attention to the plight of the homeless. American footballers J. C. Watts, Jack Kemp and Steve Largent all went into politics; so, too, did American basketball player Bill Bradley, British

Olympian Sebastian Coe and Australian swimmer Dawn Fraser, to name only a few.

But no sport can come close to matching cricket for the sheer volume of transfer into political life. If it has felt over the course of the game's history that there was a conveyor belt taking players from the pavilion to parliament, that's because at times that belt has been more than a mere metaphor. The nature of the modern game is such that the volume of transfer is increasing: there are now more active politicians who were formerly professional cricketers than at any time in the game's history, largely because embarking on a cricket career in the subcontinent is much easier if you've already acquired fame with bat or ball – and the subcontinent is where the bulk of today's cricket is played.

Yet even in previous eras, where the cult of celebrity was less developed, cricket has proved an unusually fine training ground for would-be politicians. This prompts the intriguing thought that there may be identifiably common traits in those who have made the transition – so much so that the future politicians among today's players may be guessed. More of that in a moment; for now, we can update C. L. R. James (who was himself updating Rudyard Kipling) in asking two separate but related questions: what do they know of politics who only cricket know? And what do they know of cricket who only politics know? The Authors CC game against the Lords and Commons at Wormsley provided an emphatic answer to the second at least.

It is a curious fact that no man (or woman) has yet lived who was both a great cricketer and a great statesman. In the twentieth century there were great cricketers who were mediocre politicians and mediocre cricketers who were great politicians. But we have yet to encounter a champion who has scaled the twin peaks – at least until the present day. Imran Khan is one of only eight Test players to score 3,000 runs and take 300 wickets (the top three on that list – Kapil Dev, Ian Botham and Richard Hadlee – were all his contemporaries) and stands a reasonable chance of becoming Pakistani leader, especially now that he has – in the eyes of his largely Sunni following – both stopped child-rearing with semi-Jewish girls and revived his affection for Islamic justice.

One man who reached the giddy heights of public office was Alec Douglas-Home, the only British prime minister to have played first-class cricket. In cricket as in politics, he personified mediocrity. As *Wisden*'s obituary put it: 'The general opinion is that, even if he had devoted himself to the game, he would not have been a regular County player, but then no one expected him to rise so high in politics either.' He played ten first-class matches for six different teams between 1924 and 1927, including two games for Middlesex against Oxford while still an undergraduate there in 1924 and 1925. As prime minister he was appointed by a Tory cabal to succeed Harold Macmillan, but a year later the general public sent him packing.

Most cricketers who later went into politics have been batsmen. If fielders are the lumpen proletariat of the game, and bowlers the toiling middle class, batsmen are the minor aristocracy; and perhaps their fondness for giving orders rather than receiving them explains why they have tended to be the future politicos.

Today, the number of former cricketers in politics is accelerating, and almost entirely because of batsmen. In Sri Lanka, Sanath Jayasuriya has become the first person to play international cricket after being elected to his country's parliament – distinguished from Worrell who, according to a biography, 'joined as a nominee of the government, his name put forward by the prime minister, Sir Alexander Bustamante'. Jayasuriya followed into politics the man who for many years was his captain, Arjuna Ranatunga, and they have been joined by a long-term team-mate, Hashan Tillekeratne: batsmen all. In India, Sachin Tendulkar became the fourth former cricketer – and batsman – to go into parliament when he joined the Rajya Sabha, or Upper House; though, unlike him, the other three are in the Lok Sabha, or lower house: Mohammad Azharuddin, Navjot Singh Sidhu and Kirti Azad (who also bowled brisk off-spin). Former opening bat Chetan Chauhan was also twice elected.

In the subcontinent at least, then, success on the field of cricket is fast becoming a predictor of success in politics. The fame acquired by being plastered across billboards and television channels is electoral gold; so, too, is the inevitable rubbing of shoulders with Bollywood dignitaries that comes with the Indian Premier League. Then there is the financial power. Getting into politics will cost you: India's Election Commission estimates the cost of fighting a seat is twenty-five million rupees. Only cricketers and Bollygarchs can afford that. Finally, there are the more basic affinities between cricket and politics in modern India: appalling corruption, cronyism and lack of transparency.

If this illuminates modern trends, it cannot account for the sheer weight of exchange between cricket and politics through the history of both; nor the tendency for batsmen rather than bowlers to make the leap. For that, we had better interrogate the writer Simon Kuper's claim that 'if you had to invent a sportsman to succeed in politics, it would be a cricket captain: the one sporting role that combines strategic leader with athlete', which seems right to me.

Much more than with the ninety-minute bursts of football, or even the five sets of an epic final in tennis, cricket in its purest form is the province of strategy, not tactics: it is a game whose lengthy duration is a fundamental quality. When Enoch Powell said in his verdict on Joseph Chamberlain, published in 1977, 'All political lives, unless they are cut off in midstream at a happy juncture, end in failure, because that is the nature of politics and of human affairs', he was partly reflecting on his own lengthy and turbulent career. But many political lives end very satisfactorily, and a ready and apt metaphor for them is a batsman's innings which, if it goes well, follows several distinct phases. The scratchy start, as unfamiliar conditions are navigated; the growing confidence as those conditions become familiar; the sense of potential once well set; and finally the triumph of a big score – or top job in Cabinet. The art of constructing a successful political career is an extended version of the long stay at the crease: both call on the same qualities of temperament and stamina.

In the field, too, the cricketer – and the captain in particular – must think strategically. He is forever devising plots and plans, usurpations and mischief. To the veteran observer, the air above the wicket is thick with recrimination and intrigue, just like the corridors of power. For each opponent, there is either a pre-arranged master plan or a suddenly concocted one. All real cricketers, just like all real politicians, are permanently on manoeuvres. After appearing on *Test Match Special*, Nigel Farage of UKIP was moved to write a column for the *Huffington Post* with the headline: 'Real Politicians Love Cricket'.

At the highest level, the game has often furnished its stars with genuine political and diplomatic experience. C. B. Fry was invited to be King of Albania (he declined). Tendulkar and Wasim Akram, two giants of modern Asia, made huge displays of their conviviality ahead of matches between India and Pakistan, knowing the beneficial impact it could have on reducing the chances of nuclear war over Kashmir. The D'Oliveira affair forced that batsman and many other senior players to answer diplomatically sensitive questions when he was disgracefully left out of a touring side to South Africa. Douglas-Home wanted to preserve diplomatic decency; Sir Learie Constantine described D'Oliveira's omission as 'deeply suspicious'. During the Bodyline controversy of 1932–3, MCC captain Douglas Jardine and fast bowler Harold Larwood were the centre of a major escalation in tensions between England and Australia, and didn't, at least at first, do too much to calm things down.

Even Adolf Hitler saw the game's political utility. In 1930, under the headline 'Adolf Hitler as I Know Him', the British MP Oliver Locker-Lampson revealed in the *Daily Mirror* that the Führer was taught the basics of the game by First World War POWs and thought it an ideal preparation for the mental strain of war. 'He desired to study it as a possible medium for the training of troops off duty and in times of peace,' Locker-Lampson wrote, before adding that Hitler eventually grew frustrated with the complex rules and advocated batting without pads. As patriots in battle, cricketers have always been pawns to warring nations.

But what do they know of cricket who only politics know? The world of politics seems to produce an endless supply of cricket nuts. Michael Manley, the former socialist prime minister of Jamaica, wrote a history of West Indian cricket. The image of Ken Clarke, a Cabinet minister, snoozing in the afternoon at Lord's met with little objection among the public: he seemed at home. A Cabinet minister asleep at Wimbledon or Wembley might be in more trouble; but leading politicians are rarely upbraided for indulging their love of this game. Prime ministerial Johns Major and Howard were obsessed; the former went to The Oval on the day he resigned, while the latter was nominated by the Australian and New Zealand cricket boards to be President of the ICC – who blocked his appointment – and is a director of the Foundation to preserve Bradman's legacy. David Cameron has always been a huge fan; and the devotion of another predecessor, Clement Attlee, was celebrated.

Attlee concluded his lectures on the British Empire in the early 1960s with the observation that a defining characteristic of the Commonwealth was that its constituent nations played cricket against each other. The game was, in his telling of it, the best explanation of England you could have. When he was in No. 10 Downing Street, he was adamant that there would be no Press Association ticker, or telex machine, in his office; but was finally persuaded by staff when they revealed it would also allow him to see the latest score in the cricket. Once, when Francis Williams, his press secretary, briefed lobby journalists about what was happening at No. 10, Attlee screamed at him: 'there's an account of this morning's Cabinet on my cricket machine!' Williams was never quite as frank with hacks after that.

Another man historians may look back on as a cricket nut who achieved the highest office is Matthew Hancock MP, one of the most talented and ambitious members of the Conservative intake of 2010, a group not altogether lacking in talent or ambition. Hancock gave something like a full measure of devotion to the game in setting out to play a match at the North Pole. He didn't make it there, but did play, on the Arctic plains, the most northerly game ever, before succumbing to frostbite. In another act of love for the game, he was captain and secretary of the Lords and Commons Cricket Club in 2012. In the House of Commons Register of All Party Groups, it states its purpose thus: 'To organise cricket matches for parliamentarians.'

This is a side that has always been dominated by Tories. When John Redwood was playing under the captaincy of Bill Cash, the Eurosceptic MP, he wandered into the nets without pads on, brushing aside those who said he might come to regret it. As the journalist Dominic Lawson told me: 'He was duly hit on the shin – and didn't even blink. I seem to recall that the ball made a metallic sound as it struck his bone, which made some of my colleagues gasp that he clearly was Vulcan after all.'

The side put out to play the Authors was all Tory bar one. Our fixture took place in the unspeakably beautiful undulations of Buckinghamshire, where Sir Paul Getty created an Arcadian

ground called Wormsley two decades ago. The pitch sits in a bowl
at the top of a hill beloved by huge red kites, and a set of steps
leads up to a thatched pavilion and embankment, where several
hundred spectators came to watch and bid in a charity auction for
two inspirational charities, First Story (founded by the Authors'
own William Fiennes) and Chance to Shine. The weather was
blissful. I was in captain Charlie's car for the drive, and as we
passed the sign for Stokenchurch Sam Carter said: 'I've had three
hours' sleep but I batted with the Thane of Cawdor yesterday.'
Alex Preston tweeted the remark, and within seconds one of his
followers replied saying 'I bet he's never been bowled by any man
of woman born.'

For unclear reasons your humble correspondent was promoted
to bat at number three. I had mentioned the game in one of my
columns earlier that week, noting that the last time I played with
Jo Johnson MP, when he turned out for my club Sinjuns' 2nd XI
in Wandsworth a decade earlier, the length of his run-up was in
inverse proportion to the speed of his delivery. When he came
over to have a bowl in the nets – Charlie having won the toss and
chosen to bat – he said, 'You're the chap who wrote that column
in the *Independent*, aren't you?' And not long after I answered in
the affirmative, he bowled a short one at me that had me hopping
away to leg with fear, and then – pouncing on my weakness – a
fast, full, straight delivery, to which I shouldered arms and
promptly lost my middle stump. This filled me with foreboding
when, twenty minutes later, I saw him appeal successfully to
dismiss Will lbw for seven.

And yet batting on that wicket was very heaven. No man can
say he has lived a full life until he has batted under the sun at
Wormsley. Johnson hit a fine length and moved the ball both
ways off the seam, inducing Sam to edge behind; but somehow
I found it unnervingly easy in the middle, and when the blond
Tory bowled a fullish one outside off-stump, I creamed it

through the covers. The three best sounds in all sport come in sequence: the thwack of leather on willow; the silence of the slip cordon as they watch the ball disappear; and the applause of team-mates in a distant pavilion. In a highlight of my season, I elicited all three. Even Johnson, to his credit, muttered 'Shot' in my direction.

Hancock brought himself on first change and was a joy to face. I hit him back over his head for a one-bounce four, and barely an over later set myself to do the same but pulled out of the shot at the last moment. Hardly had I noticed there wasn't a run on when I looked up to see the umpire pointing at one of those red kites, with dastardly implications for me. This struck me as curious, given I was so far down the wicket I might have shaken Hancock's hand; and the dream of a big score in front of a small crowd had died for another week at least.

James Holland then produced a magisterial innings, scoring sixty-five off fifty-eight balls in eighty minutes with a delicious range of cuts and glances and pulls and drives. He was given ample support by Charlie (14 off 17), Nick (17 off 17), Sebastian (13 off 21) and Matthew (15 off 12) but was run out by Sebastian, who went for a risky run while wrongly thinking it was the last ball before tea. He immediately apologised with all the sincerity of Mike Engleby, and we eventually ambled to 193-7 declared off thirty-five overs in two hours and seven minutes.

At tea, the charity auction produced several generous bids, and Jeremy Paxman patrolled the marquee in an excellent beige suit and panama hat, the Wormsley winds having restored to his visage some of the colour *Newsnight*'s cameras so cruelly take away. At one point, Rachel Johnson, sister of Jo and Boris, and then editrix of the *Lady*, gambolled towards him with an accomplice and said, 'Jeremy, have you met my sister-in-law Millie [Gentleman, a journalist at the *Guardian*]? She's just won the Orwell Prize.' Paxman responded that he hadn't yet had the pleasure. I took a moment, amid the scoffing of scones and family fun – there must have been fifty children there, all of them enemies of socialism – to ask the offending umpire if he was a Tory, too. 'Sport and politics don't mix,' he said. And who was I to disagree?

Johnson, who may one day be a more plausible candidate for prime minister than his older, shorter and fatter brother, opened the batting. Biff, baff, boff: he looked vulnerable early on but once his bottom hand warmed up, he flailed us to all corners for a blistering thirty-eight off twenty-six balls in just twenty-seven minutes, most of them accumulated on the leg side. But the fall of his wicket precipitated a mini collapse, and by the time they got to 98-5, with only ten overs or so remaining – three wickets to a poker-hot Tom Holland and a fine catch at slip by Sebastian – we smelt victory. Above all we were buoyed by the catch of the season, indeed the catch of any season, by Will, who starting at a wide long-off had absolutely no right to get to a skied drive. But he covered fifteen yards at full throttle, flung himself through the air like a pterodactyl on smack, and poached an astonishing catch right in front of the jubilant crowd.

By this stage Hancock had come in at number five, and the banter was getting personal. Holland (T.) reminded this close ally of George Osborne about the dire economic figures published earlier in the week. 'Where's your Plan B?' the author of *Rubicon* and *In the Shadow of the Sword* snarled. Then Plan B walked to the crease.

Here was a creature answering to the name of Shiv Haria-Shah who was so vast that he looked, as Wodehouse might have put it, as if he'd been poured into his clothes and forgot to say 'when'. Equipped with a very big bat, he and Hancock undertook the most brutal hitting assault I have ever witnessed while on the field. Far and wide these two titans smashed our attack, including one mighty six all the way past Rachel Johnson's tapenade and bruschetta and into the Pimm's tent. Together they put on seventy-five in just thirty-six balls. Hancock played some particularly delightful leg glances, with shades of Denis Compton; Haria-Shah had a violent style all of his own. But just when our heads were beginning to hang, the magnificent Nicholas Hogg – who else? – bowled Haria-Shah. His thirty-nine off just twenty-one balls in twenty-six minutes had completely changed the game; but when, two runs later, Charlie bowled Hancock, the pendulum had swung right back: 175-7, nineteen to win off sixteen balls with three wickets remaining. Then – howzat! – brilliant skill from Alex, whose glove work shone throughout the day, produced a run-out. Could we yet pull this off?

Nine to win from the final over. Charlie, who was producing an awesome spell of at-the-death bowling, was forcing the batsman to play everything. A couple of dot balls, two runs here, they've given up on the victory, a dot ball, then – howzat! – another run-out and it's a wicket needed off the last ball, with all results possible. Now the Authors, the noblest legion of literary men yet assembled on a cricket pitch, who on today of all days were playing in their glorious, Christie's-sponsored kit for the first time, huddled and high-fived like never before. The field closed in, six slips stood on their toes, Charlie came charging in and … it's a loose ball, down the leg-side, with no shot played. Alas, it was not to be.

A draw, then, with the crowd cheering us back to the pavilion and thoroughly satisfied by the drama that had unfolded. It turned out these chaps not only had a Plan B but knew a great deal about the spirit of the game and its conduct. Hancock in particular showed a deep concern for strategy, and for springing a surprise. I wouldn't want to cross him at Tory Central Office. He paced his innings astutely, gambled when appropriate, and led from the front, all of which bodes well for his political future; but his dress sense, which can only be described as a misjudged imitation of Britney Spears in the video for 'Hit Me Baby One More Time', does not. Those wraparound Oakleys, long brown shorts, rolled-up sleeves, stubby tie with fat knot and dusty loafers will have to go when he makes his bid for glory.

Talking of which, I said earlier that I would make some predictions about those within the current crop of cricketers who might go on to have a distinguished political career. All forecasters are frauds, of course. The future is unknowable. So let's have a go.

Andrew Strauss, who was rumoured to be thinking about standing as a Tory candidate in the Corby by-election after his resignation as England captain, will definitely fulfil the political potential his education at Radley and Durham University prepared him for. Kumar Sangakkara, whose seminal MCC Spirit of Cricket Cowdrey Lecture in 2011 was so brave and eloquent, will be the man to end Sri Lanka's terrible conflict. In Pakistan, it's not so much that the system is corrupt, but rather that corruption is the system: therefore expect Salman Butt to enter politics, perhaps as a minister without portfolio in Imran Khan's government. Finally, Kevin Pietersen – given his avowed hatred of 'dressing room politics' (as he calls it when texting players from the other side), his intense patriotism, charisma, diplomatic skills and fondness for social media – would doubtless make a very fine foreign secretary. For South Africa.

History has yet to give its verdict on one other character who has attempted to traverse both politics and cricket. As a child he was widely tipped for greatness, gaining entry into Surrey youth squads as a prodigious spinner of the ball, before injury curtailed his adolescent ambitions. Later he wrote a book called *Twirlymen* and starred for an Authors XI, even scoring some runs at Lord's. I contacted him for comment while writing this chapter. 'I may have taken fewer wickets than [Shane] Warne,' he told me, 'but I'll be a damn sight finer politician than [Alec] Douglas-Home.'

This was one of several games that came down to the last over, with all results possible. For the Sunday cricketers among us, matches like this are why we play cricket. The more driven players, used to regular competitive cricket, are happier grinding opponents into the dust. But unfortunately this was something we tended to experience rather than administer. Having been spectacularly caught at Wormsley by Sebastian Faulks's teenage nephew, I was only too aware of the challenge our next youthful opponents posed, and I hurriedly rang to suggest that we played the Eton 3rd XI, rather than the seconds, whom we'd been due to face.

YOUTH AND AGE

Tom Holland

Authors XI vs Eton 3rd XI, 14 June, Eton

As in love, so in cricket – youth has never been any guarantee of competence.

À la Recherche du Cricket Perdu

ow that I am forty-four, the memories I have of loathing sport as a schoolboy seem barely to belong to the seventies at all. They flicker instead with the staccato quality of old cine film, the grainy record of an age that seems almost fabulously remote. When James Joyce, in the early years of the twentieth century, wrote *A Portrait of the Artist as a Young Man*, he was looking back to the formative years of a life that had begun in 1882; but some things, it seemed to me, when I first read the novel, had barely changed since then. God knows, I will never write a *Ulysses*; but, like Stephen Dedalus, Joyce's fictional alter ego, I had certainly felt my body 'small and weak' at school, amid a throng of boys all better at sport than me. Like Stephen, I had eyes that 'were weak and watery'. Above all, like Stephen,

I had come to associate cricket with vivid childhood horrors: boredom, humiliation and pain.

'In the silence of the soft grey air he heard the cricket bats from here and from there: pock.' Prompted by the sound to wonder how it would feel to be hit, Stephen is soon contemplating the impact, not of a ball, but of something even more lethal: a 'pandybat'. 'The fellows said it was made of whalebone and leather with lead inside.' Nowadays, instruments of corporal punishment tend to be confined to specialist websites; but the provincial prep school I attended was still, even into the seventies, defiantly flying the flag for some of the more robust Victorian values. Whether the cadaverous and quite fabulously antique headmaster kept a pandybat in his own armoury, I was never unlucky enough to find out; but the knowledge that he could and would inflict pain if provoked by disobedience hung over us in our classrooms like a haze of chalkdust. The ambition of the school was clear. Arriving there the unheroic offspring of local estate agents, farmers or solicitors, we were to leave it Spartans. A sense that we were being steeled to rally the wreck of a broken square on some distant imperial frontier was never far away. Along the corridors were hung entire racks of assegais, their tips still gleaming and sharp. On rainy afternoons, when the teachers would retire to their common room and the school be given over to the boys, the more venturesome of the bullies would take down the spears and go hunting.

Nevertheless, character-building though it no doubt was to hide beneath a teacher's desk from an assegai, it was the school's obsession with sport that really made my life hell. All that possibly could have been done to make me loathe playing games with balls was done. Nothing, perhaps, makes me feel my age more keenly today than to reflect that I was alive at a time when it was considered perfectly acceptable for middle-aged men to sit puffing on their pipes, and watch naked boys share a vast communal bath after an hour or two spent on a muddy field. Cricket, it was true, did not involve getting muddy – but that was hardly a mercy. Instead of terror, it inflicted something even worse: tedium. Hour after interminable hour would be spent on the edge of a field, staring into the sky, making daisy chains and occasionally getting shouted at for fumbling a ball. Adding insult to injury, the mantra that sport existed to improve character was refined in the case of cricket to a veritable doctrine of faith. Hardly surprising, then – spurned and resentful as I was – that I should have responded with outright bolshiness. By the age of thirteen, my loathing for cricket had taken a precociously philosophical turn. Thirty years on, and I can recognise that my attitude towards the sport had become one of full-blown existentialist disdain, flavoured just for good measure with a dash of anarcho-trotskyism.

****

The child is father to the man, as Wordsworth so sagely observed. Simply asking the taxi-driver at Slough station to drive me to the playing fields of Eton is enough to set my teeth on edge. As concrete gives way to leafy expanses of green, so the years seem to fall away as well. Very deliberately, like a surgeon exploring a head wound, I probe the memories of my thirteen-year-old self. I find them surprisingly vivid. I have not reflected on them for a long while, and their intensity startles me. When you are young, and you are made to play cricket under sufferance, the balls are harder, the pitches larger, the matches last until the crack of doom. By the time the taxi turns off the road and comes to a stop, I do not just remember what it is to be nervous of playing cricket. I am nervous.

By rights, our opponents should be nothing too terrifying. Today, we are taking on a bunch of schoolboys – and a 3rd XI at that. But this is Eton. It is hard not to cringe. Walking into the pavilion, the honours boards stretch back over the entire course of the twentieth century. Here there's a Blofeld, there an Ian Fleming; 1925 boasts Lord Hyde, 1919 G. O. Allen. I love it – but I hate it, too. It is certainly no challenge now, in such a setting, to savour once again the long-forgotten flavour of my loathing for cricket. The mingled scents of wooden benches and leather cricket bags, the hang of umpires' coats from the back of a door, the arrogant clattering of studs down pavilion steps: all serve to roll back the years.

No surprise that the sight of an entire team of floppy-haired youths, larking coltishly at fielding practice and skimming in effortless throws, should make me feel my age. More unexpected, and therefore more disconcerting, is that they should make me feel thirteen again as well. Walking out on to the pavilion balcony, I look down where they are standing at fielding practice, clean-limbed and poised on the immaculate Eton turf. Pick, pack, pock, puck. Then a summons from a master. The fielding practice breaks up and the boys saunter towards a scoreboard on the edge of the pitch. One of them begins to flick a ball to and fro between his hands. As he does so, I understand with a terrible clarity that we are going to lose. The boy has the profile of Ted Dexter, and the easy, feline grace of someone who is really very, very good at sport. It is a sight that has been chilling the hearts of cricket-haters for as long as there has been compulsory sport in schools. 'grabber who is head of the skool captane of everything and winer of the mrs joyful prize for rafia work. His pater is very rich and have a super rolls enuff said.'

I make my own way over to the pitch. Charlie is already out in the middle. The toss is made and the news comes back: we will field. Instinctively, scanning the boundary's edge, I look for daisies. Naturally, of course, this being Eton, they have all been manicured out of existence. So – no daisy chains. Bearing in mind that I am now middle aged, this is doubtless just as well.

Still, it is the measure of my state of mental perturbation that I should even contemplate, decades on, the making of a daisy chain.

We shuffle out into the middle. I find myself hanging back in the rear. The instinctive flinch of the sports-hater. School days *redux*. I look around me, then over my shoulder, in the direction from which the wind is blowing. Beyond the clock tower of the pavilion, the day is turning gloomy. No prospect yet, though, of the match being cancelled. I plunge my hands into my pockets. I wait to be posted to some obscure corner of the field. I look around me again.

Hullo clouds, hullo sky.

****

There were times when my younger brother – blessed as he was with both an aptitude and a quite lunatic passion for cricket – made me yearn to be a girl, or French, or maybe both. All summer, away from school, he and my father would play out in our garden, in a makeshift net. Pick, pack, pock, puck. I, meanwhile, would skulk and malinger indoors. Had I only been named, say, Marie-Claudette, then I would not have needed to feel bad about this. As it was, though, the pressure to abandon my loathing for cricket, to answer the summons of the bat and the ball, to take up my place in the net, was a relentless one.

And like the mills of the gods, this pressure ground slow but exceeding fine. My father – who with typical perversity had abandoned golf, at which he was highly proficient, for cricket, at which he was not – provided me with an object lesson in a hitherto unsuspected truth: that enjoyment, in a sport, did not always have to depend upon excellence. As for my brother, so puppyish was his enthusiasm that it was hard even for me to stand proof against it. Indeed, over time, the sheer effort required to maintain my hostility towards cricket began to betray me. The true opposite of love, after all, is not loathing, but indifference. My very hatred had become a form of obsession.

Even so, as with Saul on the road to Damascus, so with me, it took a miracle to secure ultimate conversion. On 15 July 1981, my mother went into hospital for a routine operation, and my father, charged with looking after me, suggested that I take a punt on the Test match that was due to start the following day. 'After all,' he said, 'how can you know what you're missing if you won't even give it a chance?' The match, he explained, was at a place called Headingley, the opposition were Australia, and the person to follow was Ian Botham, previously the England captain, but now reduced humiliatingly to the ranks. With bad grace, I accepted the challenge. Five days later, by which time I had learned what a 'follow-on' was, watched Botham score 149 not out, and discovered that cricket could be the most exciting, intoxicating, heart-pumping thing in the world, I was utterly bewitched.

If there was one moment in particular when, like Benedick to Beatrice, I could say to cricket, 'I do love nothing in the world so well as you, is not that strange?', it came when I watched, for the first time on television, the hitting of a six. Down the wicket Botham danced. A swing of his bat, an opening of his shoulders, and off the ball was sent flying, straight down the ground. 'Don't bother looking for that, let alone chasing it,' as the commentary put it. 'It's gone straight into the confectionery stall and out again.' From that moment on, I wanted nothing more than to hit a six. All my former scorn was now transformed into wide-eyed obsession. For the entire remainder of that glorious, fairy-tale summer of 1981, I concentrated on making good my previous neglect. Every day was spent with my brother fathoming cricket's rudiments, and exploring its delights. After Botham had taken five wickets for one run to set up a second miraculous victory in a row, I would fantasise about bowling inswingers and leg-cutters at devastating pace. When, in the next match, he hit six sixes in a single innings, my dream of clearing the rope myself blazed with a more scorching intensity than ever. By the end of the summer, if no Ian Botham, I could at least hold a bat or bowl a ball, and in my imaginings pretend that I was.

Back at school, the news that I had become a cricketer was greeted with a mixture of hilarity and disbelief. This scepticism had a paralysing effect. Like a nervous lover, I found myself unable to perform. Tension combined with my natural ineptitude to ensure that I did not make it into any team, received no coaching and so was obliged to continue as I had begun: self-taught. Fortunately, there was another avenue. My father, after several years propping up the village 1st XI at number eleven, had retired to captain the 2nd XI, a ramshackle collection of porky veterans, gawky school-leavers and footballers impatiently sitting out the summer months. The novelty of playing as a child among men, far from inhibiting me, I found wholly liberating. If I failed, it hardly mattered – and if I succeeded, then it was all the more a triumph.

And occasionally, just occasionally, I would actually succeed. Once, for the first and only time ever, I even made it to thirty. Three balls later, after a succession of furious carves and mows, I was on forty-two. Convinced now that I had finally fathomed the secret of batting, and with my old dream of dispatching the ball straight into the confectionery stall and out again sparking across my synapses, I decided to hit my first ever six. A deep breath, a charge, a swing. A death rattle. My stumps and bails were sent flying. I could not possibly have been more out. No six, then, no fifty. Forty-two remains what it will no doubt always be: my highest ever score.

With the ball, though, I had more consistent success. Perhaps it was because good eyesight and coordination mattered that much less; perhaps it was because bowling a long-hop was never quite as terminal an error as playing a terrible shot. Either way, I began to take wickets. Twice I even took hat-tricks: once I even took four wickets in a row. I still had no idea how to bowl inswingers or leg-cutters; I still lacked the coaching that might have ironed out unnecessary kinks in my action; I still had a tendency to lose my confidence when bullied by good batsmen. But the fact remained, I was playing against real opponents, proper opponents, opponents who might well have beards, and massive forearms, and whole decades of cricket behind them, and I was actually enjoying it. I had come to realise that sport was not merely an evil conspiracy cooked up by neo-imperialist bullies to persecute people with glasses, but an opportunity even for those who lacked natural ability to feel the sheer thrill that might be derived from physical exertion and competition. The fitter and more proficient I became, so the more I came to relish it. 'Nippy wanker, ain't he?' our wicketkeeper said to my father, in an unguarded moment. How I glowed! Charging up to the wicket, bowling the ball as fast as I possibly could, revelling in the raw-red pleasure that was to be had from sending a set of stumps flying, I was not merely enjoying cricket, but something more. I was enjoying my youth.

****

Charlie does not banish me to the outfield. Instead he gives me the first over. Once, I would have accepted it as my prerogative. Now it seems more a gesture of charity. I am no longer what I was. When I run in to bowl, I feel like a biplane, creaking as I lurch, patched up with string, buffeted by swirling headwinds. No matter how hard I press down on the accelerator, it makes no difference to my speed. My confidence, unsurprisingly, is a thing of shreds and patches. I have not felt so nervous about opening the bowling since my very early teens. In cricketing terms, at any rate, I am into my second childhood.

The first ball. It is on the wicket, it is not a shocker, and it passes, to a relieved chirrup of encouragement from the fielders, into the wicketkeeper's gloves. I breathe in deeply. Five more balls. Off the very last one, with a maiden beckoning, the batsmen steal a run. Damn. Still, it could have been worse – much worse. I retreat to third man. There, in the absence of daisies, I make a study of the batsmen. Their aura of youthful invincibility, so intimidating before the start of the match, seems much diminished with them actually at the wicket. Their helmets, which everyone at school is now obliged to wear while batting, appear far too large for their necks. Their bodies, rather than appearing lithe, suddenly have the look of beanpoles. They watch the ball with a concentration so studied as to appear almost comical, their eyes saucer-wide, like those of bushbabies on the watch-out for a predatory snake. There is something a cricketer can too easily forget, perhaps, when he hits middle age: that the young can be nervous, too.

And it makes for pallid cricket. In the opening overs of the match, the balance between bat and ball is a feeble thing: a contest between two bantamweights unable to land a telling blow. Occasionally, here or there, one of the batsmen will scrabble a couple of runs; occasionally, I will get the ball to wobble past the outside edge. Thin gruel, though. Only when I am retired to the outfield for good, and Charlie brings on Nick, our best, our most bearded, our most thumpingly adult bowler, does the generational advantage abruptly swing our way. For a few brief overs, he pummels the batsmen horribly. The bushbaby eyes grow wider. Wickets begin to fall. Youth, it seems, is being put firmly in its place.

But our advantage fails to last. The bullying comes to an end. Slowly the pendulum swings back. The youthful Ted Dexter I had seen flicking the ball between his hands before the start of the match saunters out to the wicket. I am not wrong about him. Elegantly and with an immaculately tutored precision, he sets about boosting his team's run rate. By the end of the innings, our bowlers barely know where to put the ball. The scoreboard accelerates as it spins round. The fielding falls to pieces. In a telling marker of our demoralisation, more and more of my team-mates start to indulge in my own time-honoured trick, of hurling themselves dramatically on to the ground a second or two after the ball has gone scorching past on its way to the boundary. By the time we finally limp off, aches and stresses appear to be general. Even Amol, at twenty-eight our youngest player, a mere stripling, is clearly feeling his age. The young, very decidedly, have failed to show their elders the respect that is due their years.

And beyond the pavilion, the sky, much like the Authors CC, is looking grey and bruised.

****

When I became a man, I did away with childish things. As a young boy, the emotion which had characterised my relationship with cricket more than any other was, I think, an embittered resentment of those better at the game than myself. After leaving university, I sought to purge myself of the last remnants of this infant trait by a simple expedient: making myself a captain. As founder of my own team, I could, of course, take a now unadulterated pleasure in the feats and achievements of my fellows on the field of play. I could also open the bowling, station myself in the field where I would never be required to betray my lamentable failure to learn how to throw, and convey a general Brearley-esque aura of wisdom and authority. It proved a masterly strategy – and for almost two decades it delivered me sporting joy.

Then, as I neared my fortieth birthday, alarm bells began to toll. A single over of bowling, and my legs would turn to lead. Never before having taken any exercise that did not involve a cricket pitch, I now found myself facing up to an appalling realisation: I was going to have to start running round my local park. Thank God, then, for New Year's resolutions. All January I toiled. The sweat, the spumes of snot, the glistening, bright red face. Grimly, I stuck to the task. February, March, April: still I did not give up. My reward was great indeed. Come the spring, and the first match of the season, I found myself better prepared for bowling eight overs than I had ever been in my life. The summer proved a triumph. When autumn came round again, the obsession with which I now committed myself to a truly ferocious running programme had the quality of neurosis. Laps in the park had become something apotropaic.

And yet, like the habitual drug-user who finds himself taking ever larger quantities of his fix for ever-diminishing returns, as I entered my fifth decade I began to sense a decline in my bowling that no amount of boosted fitness seemed able to reverse. What had once come easily was now increasingly failing to spark. In desperation, I flogged myself ever harder. Then, a week before the start of the cricket season, I felt a stiffness in the back of my heel. Opting to ignore it, I continued with my run. By the time I was done, the stiffness had become an excruciating pain. I waited for it to heal; the pain grew only worse. One day before the first match of the season, I brought myself to consult a physiotherapist. She revealed the full scale of the damage. An Achilles tendon gone. My first serious sports injury. Out for most of the season. Only as August was starting to hint at autumn did I finally get to play again. I could bowl at last – but I might just as well not have done. I took a single wicket – and even that was a skier hit almost contemptuously into the air. And all the while, lingering above my heel, the stiffness in my tendon – a nagging hint of the dry rot of age.

And so to this season. To prepare for it, I tried one last, desperate throw, and sought what I had never had in almost four decades of playing cricket: proper coaching. Surgeon-like, the retired professional I turned to showed me how to grip the ball, how to cock my wrist, how to follow through. He encouraged me to halve my run-up. He even taught me how to throw. The flame of my self-confidence, almost extinguished, fizzed and flared back up into life. Surely, I dared to hope, in the coming season, all would be well?

It was not. In the first match for the Authors, on a skiddy artificial wicket and wearing completely the wrong shoes, my newly reconfigured run-up went disastrously to pieces. In the second match, the desperate backing that I received from my fielders resembled that of social workers encouraging a confused and incontinent pensioner to use a toilet. In the third match, I finally took some wickets; but even these failed to salve the manifold stings of uselessness, demotion and age. No longer a captain, it was now beyond me to veil my glaring incompetence in the field. Coming on second change, I had already been obliged to watch Matthew, my partner as opening bowler for well over a decade, maintain his grip on the status I had lost. And no matter that my tendon was holding up – my limbs felt so stiff, so heavy, so old! Perhaps, then, this was it: my career was ending, not with a bang, but with a whimper.

A dread which explained why, before taking a deep breath and bringing myself to make the journey to Eton, I had been ready to throw in the towel. Now the first innings of the match was over – and nothing had persuaded me to keep going with cricket. Not only was I ageing – I was retrogressing as well. Watching others on my team perform with agility, and commitment, and skill, I had felt all my old resentment of cricket, and cricketers, too, rising up from the depths of my past. As we trooped off the pitch, applauding the two youthful batsmen who had lit up the final overs with the effervescence of their batting, my mood was as lowering and tenebrous as the clouds.

And then it began to drizzle.

****

It is raining really quite hard by the time we lose our penultimate wicket and I reach for my bat and gloves. The drizzle has appeared undecided the entire length of our innings as to whether to graduate into a fully fledged downpour, but seems now at last to have made up its mind. The pall it casts over the playing fields of Eton is all too fitting. Our prospects of victory are dead. The boyish Myrmidons of the 3rd XI, with their swooping, their catching and their youthful fielding positions, have proven all too exuberant, too predatory for us. So far behind the scoring rate have we fallen that there is no longer even a mathematical possibility of us somehow snatching a victory. I might just as well not bat at all.

But I do not want to pass on what I am now resolved will be my last ever innings. I walk out to the wicket. I take my guard. I peer into the gloom. I can barely see the bowler – but from what I can make out he appears to have the casual arrogance and blond fringe of a prospective member of the Bullingdon Club. How fitting. It seems likely that my cricket career is going to end much as it began: with humiliation at the hands of my sporting betters.

Block, I tell myself. Whatever you do, just block. Do not have an abject swish and surrender your wicket without a fight. Just block.

The bowler studies the ball, flicks back his fringe, then looks at me.

Block.

He starts his run-up.

Block.

He nears the umpire.

Block, just block.

He leaps, his action graceful, his bowling arm straight. Up it goes, brushing his ear. His wrist is cocked.

Block, just block, for God's sake, just block.

Down his arm sweeps.

Block.

The ball, red and very hard, is propelled towards me, but even before it has left the bowler's fingers I have already raised my bat up high behind me, and now, as the ball blurs towards my stumps, I am planting my front foot forwards, bringing the bat down in a mighty arc, and smacking the ball, as hard as I possibly can, with the very meat of the bat. As I swing the blade up and behind my shoulder, the ball is already soaring towards the boundary, where a fielder, on its very edge, is waiting hungrily for the catch. He jumps, arms upstretched. The ball brushes his fingertips. It evades his grip. It drops into the damp grass that lies beyond the boundary rope. A six. I have hit a six. For the first time in my life, I have hit a six.

A phrase leaps unbidden to my mind. It comes from James Joyce, whose evocation of how sinister a cricket bat might sound did not prevent him, when he was old and blind, from weaving the distorted names of famous cricketers into the great phantasmagoria of *Finnegans Wake*. 'An instant of wild flight had delivered him and the cry of triumph which his lips withheld cleft his brain.'

I decide, there and then, that I will not be retiring. I will not be going gentle into that good night, after all.

As many have pointed out, cricket isn't really a team sport – as our Eton match illustrates perfectly. The rest of us slunk back to London after this bruising defeat. But for Tom, this was a moment of radiant joy. His six (Christie's Maximum, even) would be written about in the Evening Standard, *mentioned on Radio 4's* Front Row *and discussed extensively on Test Match Sofa. Furthermore, Ngayu's brilliant photos of it were shared with tens of thousands of people via Twitter. As a result, Tom would go on to win the Kevin Pietersen 'It's Tough Being Me' award for rampant egotism at our end-of-season dinner.*

CRICKET AND KIT
Charlie Campbell

Authors XI vs Millichamp & Hall XI, 17 June, Chalke Valley

> *Seven per cent of men believe they could have been professional sportsmen if only they'd trained harder.*
> From a survey by the British Heart Foundation

Tom hit that six with a Newbery GT Five Star, weighing 2lb 10oz. I know this because I chose it for him – it was a gift from the team he has run for over twenty years. For many people, including Tom, this bat is the least interesting aspect of his sporting feat. But there are many of us who place huge importance on our cricket kit, fetishising bits of leather and wood in an alarming way. We travel armed with linseed oil, bat tape and other superfluous items that are almost never required, but we feel almost bereft without them.

A builder was in my flat the other day. Surveying the mess, mostly cricketing in nature, he asked me if I was a professional cricketer. 'Semi-professional,' I replied happily. I like cricket kit and own quite a lot of it. I think it makes me better at the game. Sometimes, of course, it makes me worse – like the moment this season when I broke my beautiful custom-made bat from New Zealand and had to play with one that came from SportsDirect.com. I was promptly caught at mid-off, trying to hit over the top with that miserable piece of wood. Deep down, I probably know that it doesn't make that much difference what bat I use, but I enjoy the seriousness and symbolism of it all. There is a photo of my great-grandfather's 100th birthday party, in which my family is dressed in their smartest outfits. For me this meant my plastic suit of armour, accessorised with a sword and axe. Whites, a cricket bat, pads and gloves were the natural next step. I may not have drawn my Slazenger V12 from a stone, nor been given it by a Lady of the Lake, but my first bat was no less exciting. (It is no surprise that one manufacturer actually puts sword stickers on the back of its bats.) Like Arthur, I experienced a sense of destiny.

I learned at a young age the limitations of my sporting talent. In all my years of education, I was selected once for a school team, aged ten. In a trial, I'd impressed the coach with my fielding ability, taking a diving catch and later hitting the stumps from backward point for a run-out. And so I was selected as a specialist fielder, treading a path that Jonty Rhodes would follow five years later. But when he made the step up to Test cricket, Rhodes didn't drop five catches and make a duck in his first match. My performance prompted an onlooker to suggest the creation of a school *dis*honours board. The only thing that could have gone more wrong would have been my trousers splitting. That day taught me that I couldn't rely on innate ability to save me on the cricket field. But maybe something else could help.

Cricketers are a superstitious bunch and each player has his own rituals and routines, his own ways of ensuring success on the pitch. Jimmy Anderson has his magnetic bracelets, Jack Russell had his Weetabix and wore the same tattered sun hat throughout his career and Neil McKenzie would insist on all toilet seats being closed before he left the dressing room. Ed Smith writes in his excellent book *Luck: A Fresh Look At Fortune* about how, after the fourth delivery of every over, he would always ask the umpire the number of balls to come. (I look forward to seeing if he does this for the Authors, just as he did playing for England, Middlesex and Kent.) Amol, his rival in our middle order, always wears odd pads, one of them his, the other borrowed and never the same. Sam has a lucky cap in which he must bat – his maroon Authors one is kept for fielding. And that clearly works for him since he tops our mid-season batting averages. I lurk further down that list, and yet I own a disproportionate number of bats for a cricketer of my ability. If I include childhood and broken ones, I can count seven in my flat, four of which I have used this season. There are bargains to be found on eBay as players like me are forced by space or a new partner to have a clear-out. Only the professionals can really justify owning half a dozen expensive pieces of willow. For the rest of us it is a tremendous indulgence.

Cricket kit today is a major industry. International players are paid six-figure sums to put manufacturers' logos on their bats and clothing. Sometimes the willow they use is actually the work of another bat maker, with only the stickers being the sponsor's. But no one seems to care about this minor dishonesty. Children beg their parents for mass-produced bats that bear no relation to the handmade piece of willow they saw their hero wield – being rarely grown or manufactured on the same continent. Only the branding is the same. And the players collude in this. Having scored a century, today's professional batsmen don't salute the applauding crowd with the face of the blade – the side with which they scored the runs. Instead, they awkwardly turn the back of the bat towards the fans and cameras, so the sponsor's logo appears largest. My introduction to Test cricket was the series against the all-conquering Australian side of 1989 and I don't recall them doing this – who would have dared suggest to Steve Waugh that summer that he celebrate his centuries slightly more commercially? But by the time England regained the Ashes sixteen years later, acknowledging your sponsor in this way was common practice. And these days money dictates pretty much everything at the higher levels of cricket, and can be blamed freely for its ills.

Blame is at the core of cricket. It is a sport of more complexity than most, and a cricketer can find all sorts of reasons to explain failure. The pitch, weather or atmosphere might be responsible. It could be a team-mate – cricket sees more players dropped from sides than most sports, as a way of revitalising the team. Or maybe the opposition was unusually strong or fortunate. This season I have heard a team-mate blame a dismissal on his housing situation and more than a few players hold this book responsible for their failures at the crease. But most of us prefer to focus on our kit. As the truism goes, a bad workman blames his tools and the cricket bat is a perfect object of blame. When a player hits an effortless straight six, he attributes it to his perfect timing rather than his bat. After a horrible miscue, however, he'll stare accusingly at his willow, before playing a couple of entirely different strokes. No one knows this better than the manufacturers, who are used to the vagaries and whims of the cricketer – just as racket stringers are blamed in the world of tennis. Each player has his preferences when it comes to bats – from weight and shape to number of grains and having that bit of heartwood running down the edge of the blade. And no two bats ever feel quite the same.

Cricket bats were originally curved and resembled hockey sticks more than anything else. This was at a time when the ball was rolled along the ground towards the wicket. Cricket had emerged from a number of games, including Cat and Dog and Stool Ball, played with stones or rounded knots of wood. In St Omer a form of cricket evolved at Stonyhurst College, a school set up for the sons of Roman Catholic Englishmen who couldn't be educated in the country of their birth. Stonyhurst moved from France to Belgium, to Bruges, then to Liège, before the French revolutionary armies drove it to Lancashire. And Stonyhurst brought their version of cricket back with them – the bat resembled a long spatula and the ball was rolled along the ground at a stone wicket.

It was not until the second half of the eighteenth century that bowlers started to pitch the ball. Edward 'Lumpy' Stevens was the first great bowler to master this. He played for a number of teams, including Hambledon, and otherwise worked as a gardener for the Earl of Tankerville, who was a noted patron of the game. The name Lumpy may have come either from his ability to pitch the ball on any protrusion in the pitch, or his fondness for eating a whole apple pie at a time. With the advent of length bowling came straighter bats, with which you could play a proper defensive stroke. Bat manufacturing grew in importance – previously bats had been less expensive than balls. John Small Sr was the first-known bat-maker, and he was based at Hambledon, for whom he also played with conspicuous success. (He was also a talented musician, said once to have calmed an angry bull with a tune from his fiddle.) Hambledon also saw the famous incident when Thomas 'Shock' White came to the crease with a bat wider than the wicket. After this, the length and width of a bat were regulated, creating the shape that we know today.

For our match against a bat manufacturer, I had chosen Millichamp & Hall as our opposition. Like John Small, they are based next to a club, in their case Somerset's Taunton ground. They make bats that perform for the modern age, but with a classical appearance. They don't spoil the beautiful willow with huge garish stickers – instead you can see the grain – nor do they name their bats after warplanes or assault rifles. It is worth having a quick look at modern bat names: batsmen can walk to the wicket with a Teutonic, a Medusa, an Oblivion Slayer; or they might choose a Gladius, Anaconda or Saladin. The marketing people are dementedly pressing every button they can. M&H prefer more sober names that might equally suit the new model of Ford – Amplius or Solution. W. G. Grace made his 100th century with a Gray-Nicolls Automatic, after all.

Our predecessors were poorly equipped in comparison to us. The original Authors would have worn thin buckskin pads, gloves that provided minimal protection and bats that bore little resemblance to the modern monstrous willow, weighing up to a third less. Helmets were unheard of. Only the ball was the same. Yet they would have looked smart: stretchy, breathable clothing had yet to take over, and the combination of traditional flannels and mighty facial hair – as epitomised by Grace – is hard to beat. It is almost impossible to get old-fashioned cricket whites today, though there are still some fine beards poking through helmet grilles, with Hashim Amla possessing perhaps the best in the modern game.

Looking around the changing room, there is no one quite as kit-obsessed as me. Sam and Will, our usual opening pair, both play with Newberys – the traditionalist's manufacturer of choice – which they've owned for years. But each has runs in his locker. Just as a winning team stays unchanged, so a successful batsman rarely feels the need to upgrade his equipment. Tony McGowan is more like me – this season he has been incredibly unlucky, getting run out half a dozen times, often through no fault of his own. And while he may not be able to change his batting partners, his kit might make a difference. He's on to his second bat this season. I'm on to my third. I also found the perfect pads, which I fondly imagine to be lbw-resistant. All I need now is the ideal gloves, which I'm still looking for. The only trouble with all this superb kit is that it weighs all the more heavily on you as you walk back from the crease after a duck. You have one fewer thing to blame.

So, three days after our chastening setback at Eton, the Authors headed down to the beautiful Chalke Valley again, to play a side put together by Millichamp & Hall. We had high hopes that a scratch side of cricketers who had never met, let alone played together, would provide us with the perfect opposition against whom we could restore our confidence. After all, we had just suffered our first defeat in over a hundred years, at the hands of teenagers. But today, the opposition skipper would be selecting his bowlers and batsmen almost completely blind – relying mostly on what they said about their abilities. Last season I had thrown the ball to a bowler I hadn't played with before, who talked a good game, and I was rewarded with a twenty-six-ball over, which turned the match. And so I was hoping for something similar to happen today to the opposition.

I won the toss and put the opposition in. They were built on somewhat different lines from our teenage opponents from the last match. Two of the M&H batsmen wielded monster 3lb+ bats, and were not dissimilarly built. In another era they might have earned the nickname Lumpy themselves. Wodehouse would have said they got their money's worth from a weighing machine. This combination of size and brawn boded ill for our bowling attack. We had a few moments of promise. The ball was swinging a great deal after ten overs, and, after lulling them into a false sense of security with a rank full toss, I removed batsmen with my second and third deliveries. There is no happier moment for a bowler than when the conditions, pitch and state of the ball conspire like this, making you feel all too briefly like a threat. But a couple of long-hops in my next over were deposited in the neighbouring field and fielders spent some time searching for the ball.

During these breaks I was able to look more closely at the 3lb 4oz bat that had wrought this havoc. It had a beautiful close and straight grain, which is the most prized quality in a bat. Bat manufacturers buy their willow either directly from the landowner or from a timber agent and great judgement is needed to look at a tree, gauge the quality of the wood and agree a price, before felling. One willow tree in Essex grew to a height of 101ft and, when felled, made over a thousand cricket bats. The lowest two bat lengths of the tree produce the best clefts of wood, kept mostly for the professional game, whereas the top of the tree is generally used for making bats for children. These clefts are kept and dried for up to a year, before being shaped, pressed, shaped some more and fitted with a handle. Then the bats are sanded and polished intensively, to produce a beautiful finish. But back to the game.

The second time the fielders came back after a fruitless search. A replacement ball was procured and duly didn't move anything like as much. The spell was broken. From that moment on, things looked fairly bleak for the Authors. Batsmen came and went, but the score moved steadily over two hundred, and our wickets came mostly from catches in the deep. Our own innings started with great promise with a fine first-wicket stand from Sam and Andy Zaltzman, but, once that was broken, we lost wickets regularly and slumped to a respectable defeat. We'd fought hard, and fielded better than in any other match this season. They were just too good for us. The main consolation I had was that in a match about kit, the ball had played a decisive role. Bowlers don't just blame the pitch, the footing and their fielders and captain, but also the ball – both the condition of it and the brand. Some makes are likely to swing more than others. The MCC has stipulations about balls, including that they be designed so the shine wears off, allowing swing, both conventional and reverse.

A list from 1853 of raw materials used in ball manufacture contains some interesting entries. These include a pint of stale ale, a quarter pound of lard, half a pound of suet and Dragon's blood, whatever that may be. Ball tampering is not something confined to the modern age – at one time it was perfectly normal to grease the ball with deer fat or other such substances, to induce swing.

I am adding deer fat to my list of things the Authors require for next season – this also includes an entire tree from which we will make a team's worth of bats, so we can take the field with the unity that comes from wielding the same willow. Then all we will need is our own John Small to make these bats for us.

This match wasn't even my most chastening experience at the hands of Millichamp & Hall. They make the only set of traditional whites on the market, and I wore them to a six-a-side tournament organised by the MCC in May for its sponsors. Improbably, my team found itself in the semi-final, playing the Professional Cricketers' Association. I made my way on to the main pitch at Lord's. This should have been the high point of my entire existence, but I was aghast to find that these old-fashioned trousers had split just as I had to open the bowling to former England and Lancashire legend Neil Fairbrother. Two games before a team-mate had conceded thirty runs in an over, being hit for five sixes before having the batsman caught on the boundary's edge. Expectations were low (except with my parents, who didn't know who Fairbrother was). I didn't manage a dot ball, being hit to all parts, but I will always regard the ball that he only hit a single off as one of the finest I have bowled – the previous four having gone for boundaries. And he, like the other PCA batsmen, was playing with a Millichamp & Hall bat. I resolved to buy one.

Fortune might not have favoured us on the field but the weather gods were with us for the most part, during this wet and miserable summer. Our game against Shepperton Ladies had been re-scheduled after rain, but we were lucky enough to find another date for it. Kamila and Dan were making their debuts for us, and we were joined for this match by Hadley Freeman and her companion, Arthur. We are hoping for a greater female contingent in the Authors next season, with Scarlett Thomas lined up to play.

THE WOMEN'S XI
Kamila Shamsie

Authors XI vs Shepperton Ladies, 1 July, Shepperton

> *The occasion in the past has been very attractive to the ladies.*
> Douglas Jardine, writing about captaining
> an Authors match

1. The Walkout

I've only ever once (to my knowledge) made someone want to stage a walkout at the very sight of me. At the Galle Literature Festival, in 2008, the poet/novelist Tishani Doshi and I stepped on to the stage and an Englishwoman in the front row stood up to leave. 'I'm sorry, I must be in the wrong place,' she said. Where did she want to be? I asked. 'At the cricket panel.' This is it, I told her. Aghast, she stared up at both of us: 'But you're women.' Yes. Take a seat.

The third panellist, the cricket writer (now turned novelist) Rahul Bhattacharya hadn't yet walked on to the stage and missed this exchange. So no feelings of solidarity with his co-panellists or desire to distance himself from the view that women and cricket don't mix lay behind the statement he made later during the discussion: 'The best cricketer in India at the moment is Jhulan Goswami.'

2. An Ambrosian Figure

Jhulan Goswami, the fastest female bowler (120kph) to have played the game, has now been part of the Indian side for a decade. In 2008, when Bhattacharya made his comment, he explained that she was at the time unquestionably the best player in her field which even Sachin Tendulkar couldn't claim during that period. 'A lanky Ambrosian figure,' Bhattacharya described the 5ft 11in player. Because of the paucity of opportunities for Test cricket in the women's game, she's only played eight Tests but that's been enough to bag her match figures of 10-78 – in a game against England in which her victims included Charlotte Edwards (twice) and Claire Taylor – and a bowling average of 16.36. In ODIs, with 126 matches spanning a decade, her bowling average is 21.87 with an economy rate of 3.19. And she's handy with the bat, too. I've wanted to watch her play ever since that day in Galle, and finally thought I'd have my chance when the India and England women's teams were playing each other at Lord's on 1 July 2012. But then I looked at my calendar again. Of course. The cricketing gods can have a particularly perverse sense of humour. On that day I would be at Shepperton making my cricket debut.

3. My Life as a Cricketer Prior to 1 July 2012

4. The Coach and I

Oh, I know the game, and love it. I know and love it as a spectator. If you grow up in Pakistan not-knowing-cricket takes a monumental effort of will, a readiness to be on the periphery of the most impassioned conversations, an anti-social streak which will leave you out of the most anticipated gatherings. This is true of women as well as men, and I grew up in a world in which women were moving on from the role of 'spectator' into the world of cricket journalism. In the mid-eighties, when I fell in love with the game, the cricket magazine of choice in Pakistan – the *Cricketer* – had a female editor, Afia Salam. And one of the most respected cricket journalists in the country, also female, was Fareshteh Gati, who later played a pioneering role in uncovering match fixing in Pakistan cricket. So when there was a chance to be involved with the Authors CC and write for this book I was only following the role models I'd grown up with in saying yes. Of course, I wasn't about to play. Team manager had a fine ceremonial ring to it, I thought, and gladly adopted the title without taking on any of the attendant responsibilities. But the skipper had other ideas, and my closest friend on the team, Mirza Waheed, joined forces with him to say that of course I should play; what reason was there not to? A question to which the only answer was 'no reason at all, except that I can't'. Which was deemed entirely insufficient.

And so the day before my debut I duly made my way over to Waheed's back garden to learn grip and stance. I was resigned to being bowled first delivery, but, prior to ball's release from bowler's hand, I wanted to create the illusion that my most significant relationship to the cricket ball hadn't been that time I was so busy admiring a six hit by one of the boys in the school yard that I didn't think to move out of its way. (The mark of it remains: a tiny knot on the underside of my lip.)

So I got myself a grip. Something approaching a stance. But Waheed had decided to take his coaching duties seriously. I'll bowl to you, he said. We're going to make a player of you. He bowled the gentlest full toss the world has ever seen. I hit it. Willow on leather, that sweet, sweet sound. And in that moment

I knew that I wanted to go out on to that field at Shepperton and hit at least one ball. Even if it went straight into a fielder's hands. Just one.

5. The Debutants, 1 July

Two of us were capped that day: Dan Stevens and I. But there were two other members of the Authors CC who were inducted prior to the start of play: the Mascot, Arthur (he has a full name but a single moniker will do. Like Cher. Or Pelé. Or Lassie); and the Keeper of the Mascot, Hadley Freeman. 'Arthur sounds like Author,' the Keeper of the Mascot pointed out, and we knew it was fated. Arthur fell madly in love with the cricket ball at first sight, and spent much of the day watching it zip around before his eyes without being allowed to touch it. Oh, Arthur, I felt for you. So might a woman in other times (or, let's face it, even in these times) watch a cricket ball spin and hurtle and fly around a field of men in whites and know herself forever a spectator.

(Arthur is a Norfolk terrier. In case you were wondering.)

6. Even in These Times

Jhulan Goswami, when asked about motivation, mentioned the neighbourhood boys. 'They used to tell me, "You're a girl and girls can't play cricket." But the more they teased me the more determined I was to play cricket.' It's not just neighbourhood boys who are the problem. In the late nineties Shazia Khan, who went on to captain the Pakistan women's side, went to see Imran Khan to ask for his support in setting up a women's team. She describes how 'he sat with his feet up on the desk, and asked me why I'm bothering forming a women's team, as they will never be as good as the men's. I walked out.' And then there were the death threats from religious groups, and the warnings of riots from the police commissioner of Karachi, forcing the cancellation of the first match the Pakistan women's side was due to play. That was then. Now the Pakistan Cricket Board has a women's wing and the team is more likely to make the news for its performances (a highlight was winning gold in the Asian Games in 2010) than for any threats it receives. Imran Khan's former team-mate Abdul Qadir is Chief Selector, and Javed Miandad has provided batting tips. But funding remains low, and the world of sports is one from which many Pakistani women remain excluded in the name of social convention.

Other than the fact that I grew up in a world which designated cricket as a 'boy's sport' during the games lessons in school, I can't claim to have encountered any obstacles in my path to player – except in the wardrobe department. At the Lord's shop I was told they had run out of women's kit, and weren't sure when the next consignment was due. So it was off to Lillywhites instead. In the cricket department I looked in vain for the women's section and was informed by an unrepentant female store assistant that there was no such thing. It doesn't compare to death threats and warnings of riots, I know, but no grown woman should ever have to slink around racks of boys' clothes and discover she has the upper body of an eleven-year-old boy (I don't think so!) and the lower body of a thirteen-year-old boy (why is this so badly cut, I thought, as I tried on the trousers in the changing room? Why all this excess fabric around the … oh).

7. But Really, I'm Here to Tell You About the Match – First Innings

It was drizzling when we arrived, an inauspicious start to a match which had already been rescheduled once due to rain. That did nothing to diminish the excitement of receiving the beautiful Authors CC cap and the shirt which fortunately replaced that of the eleven-year-old boy (in the opposition's changing room, of course).

The sun broke through almost exactly as the match was due to start and the Shepperton Ladies took to the field with a warm-up routine so professional that those among the Authors XI who tried out a few competitive lunges were left looking ridiculous.

Charlie asked me where I'd like to be in the batting line-up; he suggested something up the order to ensure I had a bat; I parried with 'number eleven'; Waheed faux-huffily pointed out he hadn't given up an evening to coaching for me to go in at number eleven. A compromise was reached – Waheed would bat at eleven; I'd bat at ten. 'I hope the burden of representation doesn't affect your batting,' Waheed said.

Will and Sam opened the batting, and Sam launched from the outset into a devastating innings, interrupted only when he hit a six into the foliage and much time was spent trying to find it. He scored eighty-two with eleven fours and two sixes before he was bowled by Samantha Harvey (she later took the wicket of his opening partner, too). At the other end, Will, all watchful elegance, waited to punish the looser delivery – as can be attested by the twenty-four of his thirty-nine runs which came off boundaries. Between the two of them they put on an opening partnership of 117. I was more than slightly relieved that the length of that opening stand – twenty-one overs – made it unlikely number ten would be called upon to bat; Sam had made it look easy, but it was obvious that said a great deal more about his batting than the bowling. The chances that I would survive a single delivery let alone actually hit it seemed a very remote possibility. I didn't so much mind my team-mates knowing I was rubbish; but I really didn't want the women on the opposite side to look at me and think, because of players like that we have to deal with stereotypes of hopeless women.

Charlie was number three, and looked in great nick before he was unlucky to be given out lbw. Jon Hotten hit what was possibly the shot of the match – a backward square cut – on his way to forty-one. Dan Stevens on debut made nineteen, including two fine boundaries before he was out to the former South African international captain, Kim Price, allowing him to say the only two women who have ever bowled him over have been South African – his wife and Price. With the departure of Jon, on went Tony McGowan – and off came Tony McGowan, victim of a brilliant run-out by C. Ross. 'But it's a girl! Girls can't throw!' he cried out before sitting down to relive painful memories of the time he was the only boy in an otherwise all-girls' sixth form.

Amol Rajan swashed and buckled in typical style for twenty-three before he was out to a spectacular low catch by Chloe Russell. Despite Tony's plaintive cry it had long been obvious that the opposition was far snappier in the field than the Authors could ever hope to be. Now the wickets were falling with a discomforting regularity and, as Nick Hogg walked out to bat, I was advised to pad up. The only equipment I had were glove liners after Waheed's warning 'boys are sweaty' and the rest of the team chipped in to provide me with bat, pads, gloves. 'At least you don't need to borrow a box,' said some wag on the side whose identity I have erased from memory.

And then there was Nick, walking back to the pavilion, bowled by the fearsome Price who had already taken Amol's wicket at the start of that over, and a great cheer from my team-mates propelled me on to the field where Alex Preston appeared to be walking off in protest about something. No, actually, he was just coming over to me in order to walk me to the middle. He said something that was supportive without being patronising – everyone on the Authors' team must have had a master class in how to do this prior to my debut – and left me at the non-striker's end while he went down the other end to face the next delivery. He struck it well, and called for two immediately. But I hadn't been prepared for the bulkiness of the pads, the difficulty of running with them. One ridiculously slow run. Ground the bat. Turn for the second. 'No,' Alex called out. I was on strike.

Grip. Stance. Watch the ball. There it comes, there it comes … and that sound, what was that sound? Leather on willow, right off the centre of the bat. So delighted to have hit it, I was ready to tear off for a single without even looking to see where it had gone; Alex stopped me just as the fielder at short mid-wicket collected the ball. It didn't matter. In fact, it was all to the good. Now that I'd hit it – and hit it cleanly – I wanted to stay there and hit it again. It was the second-last over of the innings. Why not just stay there and see it through? But the sound following the next delivery was the clatter of wickets. I misjudged the pace, my bat swooshed through air, and that was it.

As I walked off, someone from the fielding side who knew I was on debut called out, 'That first one was well struck.'

I can't think of a single line in a review of one of my books that has ever pleased me so much.

Waheed was run out in the next over after some optimistic calling by Alex, and the Authors' innings ended on 244. Kim Price had figures of 4-41 including three wickets in her last over, and Chrissie Rapley ended without any wickets but with an impressive economy rate of 3.00 in eight overs.

8. But Wait, There's More – Second Innings

By now it was a glorious sunny day with a gentle breeze and blue skies. Perfect cricket weather. Aylish Cranstone and Steph Williams were the opening batsmen. Batswomen? That sounds a little strange and when I Googled the word 'batswoman' it suggested that I might mean Batwoman. Professional women cricketers seem to prefer 'batsman', so let's stick with that, passing entirely over the third option 'batter', which calls to mind either baseball or cake (the latter allowing for an unhelpful pairing of women cricketers and the kitchen).

From the start Aylish Cranstone, seventeen years old, was entirely in command, dispatching two balls to the boundary in the first over she faced. She lost her opening partner to a run-out in the fourth over, after which her scoring rate eased though no number of dot balls made her try anything foolish, no bowler seemed able to rattle her composure. I wasn't the only person in the Authors' side who, while chasing some of her shots as they sped past me to the boundary and collecting the ball off fine defensive strokes, had no doubt that one day she'd be off doing fantastic things in international cricket. Aylish Cranstone? Oh yes, I played against her.

But there was a secondary drama going on with the fielding side. A few of the players in our midst were fond of a good sledge but, unable to think of how to sledge the opposition without coming off as sexist, took to sledging each other instead. Dan Stevens had the worst of it with the Matthew Crawley jokes which he took in good humour, not even showing any signs of irritation when the first delivery he bowled resulted in a dropped catch. But if the sledging issue was easily dealt with there was another, more problematic question to be answered by men bowling at women. 'Is it wrong to bowl as aggressively as possible, or is it wrong to not bowl as aggressively as possible?' Nick Hogg asked, the question so vexing him that he immediately sent down an entirely indifferent delivery. 'Put some testosterone in it, Nick,' I advised. His second spell of bowling yielded figures of 8-1-20-2, so presumably he did.

Nine of the Authors bowled. Alex, as wicketkeeper, wasn't asked; I was asked, and refused. The batsmen were too good to be asked to put up with rank amateurishness. (Also, let's face it, embarrassingly bad batting gets you quickly out and off the field; but the worse you bowl an over the longer you have to stay there trying to get through it.) Will Fiennes took a wicket with some very fine bowling; Waheed was muttering disconsolately about the refusal of the ball to do what he wanted until he took the prized scalp of Cranstone – caught and bowled. She stayed at the crease for thirty-three overs and eighty-eight runs – which was almost exactly half of her team's final score of 180. On departure, she received the day's loudest and most admiring applause from both sides.

At a certain point it had become clear that, barring something extraordinary, the Shepperton Ladies wouldn't reach the Authors' total of 244. (Charlie was the most ungiving of all bowlers with figures of 3-1-4-1.) But merely winning on the basis of runs wasn't enough; the bowlers (all nine of them) didn't want to lose on wickets taken. The Authors had been bowled out; it seemed necessary to win by bowling the opposition out.

The chances of such a feat were looking very unlikely at the start of the thirty-ninth over with the score at 176-6. Sam was the bowler. The first delivery was a dot ball. The second a single. The third – a wicket! 'Make it a hat-trick, Sam,' I said. He laughed – 'I've never even come close' – and with the next delivery he had the batsman caught and bowled. Oh God, I thought, now he's on a hat-trick and a catch will come my way and I'll drop it. That didn't happen; the hat-trick ball posed no unanswerable questions for the batsman who dispatched it to midfield and ran a single, then turned and came back for a second ... but Captain Spectacular, Charlie Campbell, gathered up the ball and threw at the striker's end – and Alex did the rest. A hat-trick of sorts – not for the bowler, but for the team. (Is that a girly thing to say?)

Nine wickets down, one over to go. Could we get just one more batsman out? Could we?

We could not.

Result: Authors won by sixty-four runs.

9. I'm Sorry, Sam, But I Must

He scored eighty-two scintillating runs, he came closer to a hat-trick than he'd ever come before. And yet this is the moment we all talked about most: Sam fielding in the slips, a difficult catch comes his way. He doesn't take it, but crumples to the ground in the kind of agony which men reserve for a particular kind of hurt. All his team-mates rush to his side, other than one. The only woman on the team finds she is walking over to the two other women on the field instead even as the umpire cries out to her 'That's your entire chapter, right there!'

'I hear that hurts,' says the only woman on the team as she and the two women with bats in their hands watch the man lying on the ground in foetal position.

'I thought about apologising,' said the woman who had struck the ball. 'But he really should have caught it.'

10. How the First Women's Cricket Match Was Reported

> *'Eleven maids of Bramley and eleven maids of Hambledon, all dressed in white.'*
>
> *Reading Mercury*, 26 July 1745

11. We've Come So Far, and Yet

When writing about Jhulan Goswami at the start of this chapter it didn't occur to me to wonder if I should explain what 'an Ambrosian figure' is. Anyone who knows anything about the game would know I was comparing her to a West Indian fast bowler, not the nectar of the gods. But did I need to explain Charlotte Edwards and Claire Taylor? Oh surely not. Would you need to explain the Williams sisters to someone who knows Roger Federer, or Martina Navratilova to anyone who's ever heard of Björn Borg? But the gaping deficit in the analogy I'm trying to draw points to just how far women's cricket still needs to go to enter the public consciousness, even while the example of the women tennis players serves as reminder of how much the viewing public has to gain if sponsorship and media coverage and training facilities bring the women's game to the foreground.

And let me admit this here, at the end, in the whisper of a confessional: I had never seen women cricketers play until that day at Shepperton.

It was at this point in the season that the weather became truly atrocious. Rain blanketed the country and there appeared to be no prospect of cricket for the next month. Our long-awaited game at Arundel Castle fell foul of the weather, heartbreakingly. Former Sussex captain Johnny Barclay had generously invited us down but what the gods give, they can take away. The prospect for our game at the spectacular Valley of Rocks in north Devon looked equally bleak. But our opponents (who wouldn't have to drive four and a half hours each way) were sanguine and we decided to give it a go. It was at this point that the cautious brigade made themselves known. It was the non-fiction writers who called and texted the most to check that the game was still on. But we pressed on past Bristol, praying that the pitch inspection would be favourable, and the phone wouldn't ring with the news that there'd be no game.

CRICKET AND MEMORY

William Fiennes

Authors XI vs Lynton & Lynmouth CC, 8 July,
the Valley of Rocks

And the burned batsmen returned, with changed faces,
'Like men returned from a far journey,'
Under the long glare walls of evening ...

Ted Hughes, 'Sunstruck'

The wettest summer for a hundred years, the wettest June since records began, and this Sunday morning – the rain a car-wash deluge on the windscreen, too much for wipers to deal with – cricket seemed a dream someone once had in another country, a long time ago. But I reached the Severn plain as if coming out from beneath a canopy of water, the sky bright and clear, and after I'd picked up our wicketkeeper-novelist Alex from Taunton station it was unimpeachably summer, windows down, ears popping on the north Devon uplands west of Minehead, across the open moors among estate cars topped with surfboards and cycles, into dark-wooded combes on narrow, vertiginous roads with signs boasting the gradients and escape lanes that made brake failure a vivid possibility in the mind's eye.

Already a weight of cricket season gathering behind us: that all-weather strip in Victoria Park, both teams huddling beneath a cherry tree against the rain. Blossom on the cherries then, leaves just emerging on the London planes, an outfield of muddy goalmouth craters patrolled by crows, the Clapton Park Estate towers rising in the distance. Collecting Waheed and Nick from Hammersmith, Ngayu straight from a shift at the hospital, laden with tripods and lenses. The Crystal Palace and Croydon transmitter masts above the Trevor Bailey Sports Ground in Dulwich, parakeets flouncing out of Sydenham Hill Wood. The journey to Chalke Valley in Wiltshire, heads so full of cricket that even the Stonehenge trilithons looked like designs for wickets, lintels lying like bails across the vertical stones. The red kites at Wormsley in its bowl of woodland. Aylish Cranstone's swivel-pulls; Clare Ross's stump-top miracle throws; Tony in his knee brace, flipping his cap off whenever he turned to chase the ball. The talk of bats – Charlie's Laver & Wood dispatched from New Zealand, Sam's Newbery 'Navarone' carrying an occult power like Prospero's staff, the weather-beaten SG that Amol seemed to have been using continuously since his eleventh birthday.

Over Porlock Hill, Countisbury Hill, Foreland Point, the hog's back cliffs of north Exmoor, cumulus shadows cruising the Bristol Channel towards Bridgend and Swansea. Queues at the seafood stalls in Lynmouth, surfers waiting in the Blacklands break. We climbed a steep switchback, passed through Lynton, crossed a cattle grid in a dark tunnel of trees. And then we were somewhere else entirely: at the head of a deep, scooped valley, ridges to left and right finished with craggy stacks and boulders, the sea at Wingcliff Bay glittering in the distance. A few black and white Cheviot goats picked through the bracken, Exmoor ponies grazed a paddock-like clearing, and there below us, centre of the frame, lay the tidy fenced-in flatness of a cricket ground, a gull waiting at one end of the wicket like an umpire.

****

I liked the music first, Booker T & the MGs playing 'Soul Limbo' before Richie Benaud and Peter West introduced the Test matches on BBC2. Eight years old, last days of the summer term, I'd come down with a temperature and pox-like blisters the doctor called impetigo. Infectious, I had to stay away from school, so I lay in bed with the summer going on outside, a floaty sensation as the fever broke, a district nurse arriving to dress the wounds, scabs like small coins scattered across my trunk and legs and arms. I remember the smell of gauze Melolin dressings, the coolness and pink chalky crust of calamine lotion, my mother squeezing oranges and stirring in glucose powder for a sweetness that seemed more restorative and remedial than sugar's. And on the little portable TV with its wire halo aerial at the foot of the bed I followed a cricket match from start to finish for the first time. England vs India at Edgbaston, 1979. England amassed 633-5, David Gower scoring 200 not out, no helmet, his long-sleeved billowy white shirt unbuttoned further than strictly necessary. He was twenty-two and had made his England debut the previous year, his batting an enterprise of touch and timing rather than brute force. I never forgot that innings, its grace and fluency, its pure style, and Gower (followed closely by Kapil Dev, who took all five wickets in England's innings) became my first sporting hero as the nurse arrived in her starched white dress, Mum bringing cold Ovaltine, or toast and Marmite, the doctor in his tortoiseshell glasses, the cold medal of the stethoscope on my skin. I came under the spell of the game I'd seen my father and brothers follow on television, men in white clothes moving in mysterious patterns across the green.

I got my first bat for my birthday the following year. The Gray-Nicolls double scoop David Gower used was too expensive, but I rubbed linseed oil into my Gunn & Moore with devotional care. At school we wrote letters to bat manufacturers, requesting stickers, so Slazenger panthers and the black and white Duncan

Fearnley wicket designs like badger faces proliferated across our desks and lockers and tins. We couldn't run anywhere without breaking into imitations of bowling actions – Graham Dilley's cantilever front leg, Bob Willis cranking his arm behind his back like a pump handle, Terry Alderman, Ian Botham – because by then we'd lived through the Ashes series of 1981, when my father had taken me to Edgbaston and we'd seen Botham's spell of 5-1 in twenty-eight balls and England win the match by twenty-nine runs. When we went to Lord's the next summer I took an empty plastic film canister, filled it with grass from the outfield and kept it like an urn of ashes on my bedroom window sill. I'd ask for the latest *Wisden* for Christmas; I started keeping wicket, because my father had; I read Godfrey Evans's *Wicketkeepers of the World*, Viv Richards's *Sir Vivian*, Mike Brearley's *Phoenix from the Ashes*, even *Frindall's Scorebook 1978–9: Australia vs England*, which was basically just a copy of Bill Frindall's idiosyncratic score sheets, pages of numbers and strange glyphs from which you could reconstruct passages of time in novelistic detail. And from April through until September I waited for my father to come home from work so he could bowl at me on the lawn, dropping his jumper on the grass to mark a crease. Past sixty, he bowled round-arm or threw the ball down again and again so I could rehearse particular shots – forward defensive, square cut, cover drive, sweep – trying to move my feet according to the approved historical blueprint, left foot forward to the pitch of the ball, right foot back and across for the cut, oak trees and cattle in the fields behind my father, parties of swifts screaming above us in the dusk.

Even then I must have been internalising some sense of a classical ideal, a perfection of form, those repeated instructions – straight bat, head over the ball, lead with the top hand, left elbow high – gathering the force of moral imperatives. Somehow I had to close the gap between the grace of movement I could see in my mind's eye and the imperfect figure I made in the world. There was a lovely feeling of mastery and power when that gap narrowed or even disappeared in a cover drive, left shoulder leading the body's weight towards the ball, left hand guiding the bat towards and through the line, maker's name showing on the follow-through – a feeling of *rightness*, as if I'd found the only possible answer to a question in the moment it was being asked. I was proud when Dad recognised it, too, and cheered.

****

The Valley of Rocks. Even the name sounded epic, mythical – maybe it was the valley in Leonardo's *Virgin of the Rocks*, the holy figures posed in a brooding landscape of crags, stacks and columns. Nineteenth-century accounts referred to circles of druidical stones in the valley; local myths spun an actual castle from the massive sandstone tor known as Castle Rock, haunted by a monk in a black robe. Real adders thrived in the bracken.

The Lynton & Lynmouth Cricket Club had been founded by a Captain Hume in 1876 'to cater for the welfare of the young men of the neighbourhood'; in 1891, the Lynton benefactor Sir George Newnes paid for Warren Field in the Valley of Rocks to be levelled for a cricket ground. Newnes was forty, the son of a Congregational minister in Derbyshire. He'd settled in Manchester with his wife, Priscilla, and started a cheap mass-market magazine called *Tit-Bits*, which soon had weekly sales of 700,000. Among other publishing ventures, Newnes would launch the *Strand* magazine, where Conan Doyle's Sherlock Holmes stories first appeared; he'd become Liberal MP for Newmarket in 1885, fund the Free Library in Putney and an electric tramway in Matlock, and serve as President of the British Chess Club. But Lynton was the focus of his largesse. He visited the town on holiday in 1887, built himself a mansion on a hill – Hollerday House – and paid for the Town Hall on Lee Road, a new Congregational church, the water-powered funicular railway linking Lynton and Lynmouth, and this cricket field *Country Life* would later call 'the Queen of English cricket grounds' and *Wisden* feature at number two in a list of the most beautiful grounds in the country.

Surely it was a kind of madness – to pitch an enterprise demanding flat, clear spaces on to a landscape defined by rock, combe, cliff and gorge. I thought of Fitzcarraldo dreaming his opera house in the rainforest, hauling the steamer over the hill. Castle Rock loomed in the mouth of the valley; other stacks and tors notched the skyline: Rugged Jack, Middle Gate, Chimney Rock, the Devil's Cheesewring. The pavilion, couched in a stand of sycamores, had a bunker solidness, with wooden awnings that lifted on iron arms over the windows, and a swallow's nest immediately above the front door, a swallow slotting into it like a key.

Spirits lifted, arriving in such a place. But the Lynton & Lynmouth XI included several players aged eighteen to twenty-five, and this was a bad sign. I'd overheard them discuss how they wanted to bowl first, give the wicket an extra three hours to dry out in the sun – Charlie would have done the same but he lost the toss, so Sam and I were putting our pads on, trying to gather our capacity for steadiness of attention after five hours on the road, the flicker and hurtle beyond the glass. My scores – thirty, thirty-four, thirty-nine – had been growing, and I was hopeful. I longed to make fifty, just once, this season. I relished walking out to bat with Sam, who really knew what he was doing. We'd put on eighty at Chalke Valley, and 117 at Shepperton – partnerships in which I'd played a conspicuously beta role. Sam batted with such decisive intent and authority, he struck the ball so cleanly, I'd grown used to watching from the bowler's end as his cuts, drives and clips sliced the ring and thrashed into perimeter fences and undergrowth. Meanwhile, my forward defensives had textbook shape, and I left the wide ones outside off-stump with a kind of toreador lift of the arms, but the dot balls assembled in platoons. Sometimes I felt I wasn't having any luck, watching as bowlers fed Sam half-volleys and wide long-hops, while I'd get successions of straight, good-length balls, no easy hits. But it wasn't luck. Sam's will to score unnerved the bowlers and *forced* the loose stuff, while my meekness filled them with confidence. I only had myself to blame.

I wanted some of that run-making power. I thought maybe the secret lay in a lucky cap like Sam's, hooped in an old Sussex club's blues and pinks, or the way he tapped his bat to his guard in bursts of three as the bowler approached, a quick Morse signature so distinctive that blindfolded I'd have known Sam was taking strike. I wondered if as a boy playing on the lawn with my father, or as a schoolboy cricketer, I'd become too attached to the idea of correct form, worrying more about the shape I made in the world than the effect I had on it. This wasn't the only province of my life in which I wished for less refinement, more fire.

****

I carried my father's instructions and the idea of grace with me whenever I walked out towards the wicket. Groundsmen roped off the cricket square on the school playing field as if a crime had been committed there, tractors dragging gang mowers back and forth, slipstreams of dust and chaff like heat hazes behind them. I remember the wooden thatched pavilion, peat-brown, with its splintery floor and smell of creosote and leather, the slip-catching cradle by the war memorial – the curved ash spars sitting like the hull of a boat in wrought-iron dry dock – and how sometimes, if you threw it just right, the ball followed the curve of the spars as if shooting a groove and flew out towards your partner with new speed and character. In breaks we raced for games of playground cricket, stumps chalked on the cement between bricks, a dustbin marking the bowler's end. I remember the singe-smoke of magnifying glasses burning initials into tennis balls, a drain

known as The Orinoco from which balls emerged with a rank
sewagey coating, and pricking numbers into the sides of pencils
with compass points for elaborate Owzthat games featuring teams
of our friends against Rest of the World XIs, Sunil Gavaskar
opening the batting with Gordon Greenidge. After school we'd
run down to The Parks, where the University XI played three-day
matches against first-class counties, which meant we might catch
glimpses of Joel Garner, Mike Proctor or Derek Randall. We
roamed the perimeter with our autograph books, and when
Worcestershire's veteran spinner Norman Gifford picked me up
and carried me towards the wicket, in among the circle of fielders,
I felt suddenly transported into a grown-up enchanted world I'd
only seen on television.

My mother had played cricket, too – she'd been captain of her
school team, an achievement Dad never took very seriously – and
sometimes she'd bowl to me, underarm, or throw the ball down
from three yards away so I could rehearse my forward defensives
and off drives, always trying to recreate in the day the perfect
shapes I could see in my head. But cricket was my father's
hinterland. He saw his first proper match in September 1928, at
The Oval, watching Lancashire (the 'Champion County') take
on The Rest, including Hobbs, Sutcliffe, Woolley, Hammond,
Ames and Larwood. In 1929 the family moved to St John's
Wood, and after lessons Dad's governess, Miss Clarke, might take
him to Lord's to watch Middlesex, the two of them sitting in Q
Stand as the Revd E. T. Killick opened the batting, Jack Hearne
and Patsy Hendren at three and four. Dad cut photos of cricketers
from newspapers and glued them into scrapbooks. They spent
summers at Brighton, where a Test match scoreboard, sponsored
by Johnnie Walker, went up near West Pier, and Dad and Miss
Clarke joined the crowds gathered in front of it to follow the
action from Lord's, K. S. Duleepsinhji making 173 for England
before Bill Woodfull (155) and Don Bradman (254) helped

Australia to 729-6 declared. Much later, whenever we went to Lord's together, we'd bump into old friends of my father's who'd tell me how good he was at cricket, a real talent, if only the war hadn't got in the way. Mum has a photo of him batting at Lord's in August 1939, Lord's Schools vs The Rest, eighteen years old, three weeks before the war began, and whenever I look at it I think of what was coming and that small, safe world within the boundary. When Dad holds his hands up I can see his fingers all crooked from wicketkeeping; when he takes an apple from the bowl he can't help lobbing it up and catching it, whipping off the bails, and if he's putting a ladle or wooden spoon back in the kitchen drawer he can't help but hold it with both hands, a straight back lift, clip the ball off his hips or push it through the covers. He doesn't think anyone's looking.

****

They don't cover the wicket at the Valley of Rocks and after so much rain the strip might have been laid directly on the water table. The wicket is sluggish and doughy, the bounce unpredictable, and Lynton's bowlers, led by club captain Nick Constable, student James Thomas and stonemason Alex Spice, keep a tight line and length. You've got to concentrate: I remember something Mike Atherton said about watching not just the ball but the *seam* on the ball. It's not just me: this really is hard to bat on. The outfield is sodden and slow; even Sam is constrained to singles. I manage a few glances to fine leg, back-foot pushes past cover, a pull behind square leg for four, sometimes gazing from the non-striker's end at Castle Rock and Wingcliff Bay, black and white Cheviot goats stepping up on to sandstone slabs as if on to podiums, our calls – Yes! No! Wait! – rolling round the amphitheatre of rock and bracken as Ngayu climbs to Rugged Jack for a bird's eye vantage. Sam starts to find the boundary, getting into his groove, and at the drinks break after twenty overs we've built a partnership of seventy-seven, of which I've scored a paltry fifteen. But it's been such hard work, the surface so challenging to bat on, this seems a pretty good effort: close to four an over, ten wickets in hand. Commentators would be talking about 'a platform'.

Still, I'm embarrassed. Fifteen off twenty overs: I mean, *come on*. I've got to speed up. Straight after drinks, Nick Constable brings on a new bowler, an eighteen-year-old named Laurence May. You can tell he's a serious cricketer, he's bowling faster than the others, with a smooth, powerful action. But even as he approaches the wicket I've decided to hit big. I'm going to clout it back over his head into the sycamores, strike it long over mid-wicket towards the Exmoor ponies. I'm seeing this other self in my mind's eye, full of confidence and power. The ball comes straight and full, I swing the bat, I hear the disappointment-rattle of stumps and bails, and it's from the pavilion bench that I watch Sam shift gear, hitting student Jezza Bingham for twenty-eight off two overs, with three sixes, before May gets Sam too, bowled for seventy-five. And then the Authors are in trouble, the next five batsmen knocked over for 0, 2, 9, 5 and 1, with only Nick Hogg getting stuck in, contributing thirty-one not out to an Authors total of 176-7 after forty.

It takes me by surprise, how competitive I feel just now, as we collect mugs of tea and load plates with cheese and pickle sandwiches and half-scones blobbed with clotted cream and strawberry jam. A hundred and seventy-six – it's not much, but we're in it, the wicket's so tricky, the strip messy with bowlers' foot holes. If we can keep it tight, maybe Nick can make an early breakthrough, or Charlie can find the freaky inswing that skittled those two Millichamp guys in Wiltshire, or Devon-based novelist Tom Vowler, on debut, will turn out to be a bowler of unplayable expertise. We run back out on to the soggy ground.

Nick Constable's sons Lewis and Conor open the batting. Nick Hogg gets Lewis early, bowled for two, and then bowls his replacement Jezza Bingham for four. Lynton are 22-2, Hogg's got 2-5 off three overs, and I can't have been the only one thinking we could win it. I'm at cover, walking in. I want to do my bit. I want to stop everything, throw myself full-length if necessary. It wouldn't hurt – this ground is so damp, I'd just slide across it, no problem – and those extra two or three runs could make all the difference. But then Laurence May, who's toured South Africa with the Devon youth team, comes in to join media student Conor Constable, who promptly plants his foot and sends the ball sailing into the bracken by the Devil's Cheesewring. May doesn't seem bothered by the spongy wicket. He makes it look easy, smashing the two historian Toms over the top, or through the covers, between me and Sam, connecting with one square drive so sweetly I don't even think about diving for it, it's already gone. And then a few balls later May plays the same stroke, and everything changes.

The ball's travelling past me, to my left, within range, and I want to stop it. It's not a dive, exactly, more a sort of lunge-stumble that gets my left hand down to the ball, and for a split second I'm glad I've saved a run, glad to feel the youth-residue of throwing myself across grass to stop a cricket ball. But momentum carries my body onwards, over the top of the ball, and I land not on my outstretched arm but on the angle of my shoulder, and the ground's so soft after all the rain that instead of sliding on top of it my shoulder ploughs through the turf, driving into soil, the brunt of impact ramming through my collarbone.

Later, Nick and Tom would say they heard the snap, like someone treading on a stick. I've never broken a bone before, but when I run my finger along my collarbone I can feel it, something jagged poking under the skin. I can't move my left arm. The pain kicks in. My team-mates gather in a circle above me, the closest they've come to a huddle all season. Ngayu comes down from the crags, looks at my shoulder and says, 'Oh fuck.' And then Charlie is driving me to A&E at the North Devon District Hospital in Barnstaple and I am feeling ridiculous, sitting in my whites and cricket boots in the crowded waiting room. Vending machines and prams, a TV mounted just under the ceiling. Roger Federer has beaten Andy Murray in the Men's Final at Wimbledon; the line judges, the ball boys and girls, stand at the net, hands behind their backs; a shoal of camera flashes passes through Centre Court as Federer raises his golden trophy. I try to tell Charlie to go back to the game, I'll be fine, but he insists on staying. Murray takes the microphone from Sue Barker and congratulates his opponent, his voice cracking. The crowd cheers and applauds. Murray keeps pausing, on the brink of tears. He thanks his team, and then the spectators. 'Everybody always talks about the pressure of playing at Wimbledon,' he says, 'how tough it is, but it's not the people watching, they make it so much easier to play.'

I know my season's over. No match at Lord's, or Hambledon. My studs clack on the floor on the way through triage to the curtained cubicles. The X-ray shows a fully displaced clavicle fracture. Months, not weeks, before I play cricket again. I might need a titanium plate, pins, screws. Meanwhile, at the Valley of Rocks, May and Constable are having a ball. Constable goes for fifty-nine, but May makes 106 not out, with seventeen fours and two sixes. Lynton & Lynmouth CC finish on 179-4 off twenty-nine overs. Two nurses called Sarah give me liquid morphine by mouth, support my arm in a navy blue poly-sling. I lie back as the Oramorph takes over. Sarah and Sarah wear blue V-neck scrubs. Outside the cubicle, a drunk man with a bandage round his head shouts at the registrar. One of the Sarahs moved to north Devon from the city; she cycles across the moors at weekends. I feel light, as if I could float. I think of Lorna Doone, druids chanting round the standing stones, that morning's downpour, how far away it all seems. Then I'm at Wormsley, running in from long-off, the ball soaring towards me on its long parabola. The white marquees gleam like sails. My mother and father watch from the deckchairs. The ball falls and keeps falling, and I keep moving towards it, reaching.

Will had been heroic up until this point. The best fielder in the side and the most stylish batsman, he was a stalwart of the Authors, driving people uncomplainingly to matches, keeping wicket when needed and forming the ideal opening partnership with Sam. We had a gloomy month, waiting for news of his collarbone, with very little cricket to alleviate things. We had a good game against the Thespian Thunderers, a very likeable side of actors, in which Nick took five wickets and children's author Joe Craig announced himself with a fine forty-eight. But we had to wait until August for our long-awaited match against the Publishers.

CRICKET AND BOOKS
Sam Carter

Authors XI vs Publishers XI, 10 August, Dulwich College

Even cricketers can be extremely stupid about the value of books.
C. B. Fry

'Cricket and words seem to go together,' said Beryl Bainbridge. She was right, of course.

The Authors XI are liquid-lunching in the Bat & Ball prior to our game at Hambledon, the cradle of cricket, and historian and miserly medium-pacer Tom Penn is loosening up on the subject of that seminal work *The Young Cricketer's Tutor*. Its author, John Nyren (son of the old landlord of this pub), was the Adam of cricket writers. Before his arrival, cricket books had been dry compilations of scorecards and fixtures, or instruction manuals. With *The Young Cricketers' Tutor*, Nyren made the ambitious presumption that out there was a readership interested in the personalities and characteristics of cricketers, in his case the champions of the famous Hambledon Club during their brief time in the sun. His early Victorian readership vindicated him spectacularly, and cricket literature was born.

For a century the Authors Cricket Club lay largely fallow until revived in 2012 by Charlie and Nick, but the absence of an 'official' team of writers had no discernible effect on the number of cricket books arriving on the shelves. There is now more literature on cricket than on any other sport, and still it comes: biographies, autobiographies, the annual *Wisden*, coaching manuals, ghosted diaries, hurried celebrations of great victories, revisionist tracts, whimsical reflections ... No aspect of cricket has escaped an obsessive's pen, from the gloomy subject of cricketing suicides to the advent of sledging.

Sports books have never enjoyed the highest of reputations; they never win literary prizes and are often passed over with a sneer when the great and good pick their 'books of the year'. But cricketers and cricket writers have always flattered themselves that they operate on a higher plane, that they can raise their prose to the level of literature. Myriad theories abound to explain the unique richness of cricket writing, or maybe simply to rationalise and justify the obsession. For some the explanation lies in the reflective nature of the game and the subtle rhythms within. For others the wellspring of this plenty is the acute existential crises of cricket. Yet more draw a comparison between the essential loneliness of both the writer and the cricketer. Or perhaps it's just something to do with the sheer amount of time it all takes?

So what makes it into the canon of cricket writing? Roald Dahl's character Uncle Oswald never travels without his 'box of books', thus he is inoculated against fate and boredom. When the lothario's Lagonda breaks down and he finds himself stranded in the Sinai Desert, Oswald reaches in and plucks out a volume at random: 'The box contained thirty or forty of the best books in the world, and all of them could be reread a hundred times and would improve with each reading. It was immaterial which one I got.' A sort of analogue Kindle, I suppose.

Which cricket books, which cricket writers, might vie for a place within that box? Could any cricket book stand rereading a hundred times (as students we certainly watched the *Botham's Ashes* video that often)? One book invariably tops every poll taken of 'best cricket book' (and, indeed, often best sports book): C. L. R. James's *Beyond a Boundary*. Unashamedly literary Trinidadian Marxists are rarely lauded by the egg and bacon MCC brigade, but James is the exception. His masterpiece was published in 1963, an intriguing mix of autobiography, history, philosophy and cricket. James's complex and subtle work meets that test of 'improving every time' and passes it triumphantly. Few writers can draw us in so completely and make us share the victories and failures of long-dead heroes. The resonance of his physical descriptions (Wilton St Hill has 'forearms like whipcord') match the depth of analysis of the social significance of pioneers like Constantine, Headley and Worrell. The genius of this work lies in its vaulting thematic scope – 'what do they know of cricket who only cricket know?' it asks. Here you find the most nuanced and personal examination of the colonial condition and the account of James's campaign to appoint the first black captain of the West Indies, with its gloriously happy ending. And there is James flattening some thoroughly deserving targets (West Indian brilliance on the cricket field due to easy 'spontaneity') and lambasting the social historians who would presume to write English history without due prominence for W. G. Grace. Most ambitiously, he mounts an elegant argument that cricket is indeed art, though at this point even his most ardent admirers blush slightly and look down at their shoes.

C. L. R. James came to England in 1932 to join his friend Learie Constantine, at the time playing for Nelson in the Lancashire leagues. James got his break in cricket journalism from Neville Cardus of the then *Manchester Guardian*. Cardus, who combined the roles of music critic and cricket correspondent for the paper, is another evergreen selection for the Best Cricket Writers' XI. Known for an unrestrained ripeness of prose ('The brevity in Woolley's batting is a thing of pulse or spirit, not to be checked by clocks, but only to be apprehended by imagination'), Cardus often studded his cricket writing with musical metaphors. However, he held back from reversing the trick when writing his review of the Hallé Orchestra's performance of Beethoven's Ninth. C. L. R. James would have had no such qualms. J. B. Priestley endorsed Cardus's famous memoirs, half on cricket and half music, thus: 'It is the best autobiography I have read since Hitler began taking Europe apart.' Cardus reaches back to the lyricism of Nyren, and both for good and ill defined the abiding characteristic of cricket writing: nostalgia. Those who took up the baton include R. C. 'Crusoe' Robertson-Glasgow, Alan Ross and John Arlott; all brought a poet's sensibility to their descriptions of the game. Then there are the chroniclers, the completists and the statisticians. *Wisden* is their bible and the prolific F. S. Ashley-Cooper ('the Herodotus of cricket') their high priest.

Publishers want bestsellers, and the days when a cricket writer won a book deal on the basis of lyrical prose or mastery of stats were numbered. In my childhood, as now, the most popular cricket books were the autobiographies of the leading players and accounts of great series. 'In summer you play cricket and in winter you read about it,' said Robert Menzies. Hooked on the game, but a better reader than a cricketer, I would devour these tomes, but few stand up at a distance of time. Rarely the famous cricketer escapes the dead hand of the 'and then I played for Essex U12s … and then I played for Essex U13s' school of writing, or avoids the relentless and humourless self-justification that lies within those glossy covers. Axes grind and old scores are settled on every page.

Surely the least one can expect of a cricketer who ventures into print is that he has read some books himself. The endless hours on the tour bus, in the hotels and in the dressing room. Wishful thinking. The excellent modern writer Gideon Haigh has a telling tale for those with high expectations of the professional cricketer as writer. Kept waiting for a promised interview with Shane Warne, Haigh passed the time with the book he had on the go, a study of a devastating early twentieth-century hurricane and the origins of scientific weather forecasting. When Warne rocked up he asked the journalist what he was reading. On hearing the answer, Warne paused, nodded and said: 'Yeah, I read this book once … it was about UFOs.' In fairness, Haigh actually tells the story for two reasons: to illustrate Warne's engaging friendliness, and to expiate his own sin of snobbery.

But read with close attention even the most banal of autobiographies yields up a hidden gem or revelatory moment. Happily, perhaps because cricketers are less ruthlessly controlled and managed than their footballing brethren, their books always have the potential to surprise, like the delivery that suddenly rears from a length off a placid pitch. It's an indelible cliché that, due to the nature and duration of a cricket match, a player's true personality will come out in his play. Perhaps it inadvertently emerges in his books, too.

Mike Brearley has a reputation as the most cerebral of England captains, gentle of manner and handshake. His Australian counterpart Kim Hughes's sledge, 'nothing going for him except that he was intelligent', has become the Authors' motto. But read Brearley's books carefully and you see that the mailed fist was never far beneath. We're in Australia in 1978/9, and England have to deal with the potentially catastrophic problem of strike bowler Bob Willis missing Tests through injury (his old cobbler has retired and, on the unyielding baked pitches, the new boots have shredded his feet). Sympathy from the skipper for the mop-haired beanpole is scant – Willis is to soldier on and then have a few of the septic digits amputated only after England have retained the Ashes.

But Brearley could be most generous to his team-mates, too, even the most angular among them. He did, after all, have a 'degree in people'. Here's an oft-quoted paean to the complex Geoffrey Boycott, captured as he weaved amid a Rodney Hogg barrage: 'As I stood at the non-striker's end, and watched him avoid yet another hostile ball, I felt a wave of admiration for my partner; wiry, slight, dedicated, a lonely man doing a lonely job all these years. What was it that compelled him to prove himself again and again among his peers?'

Brearley leaves the question hanging. Boycott himself, unconsciously, gives us some answers. A different book, a different tour. England are playing a warm-up game in Malaysia on their way to Australia again, and as Boycott comes off the field the local scorer, a girl who has been doing duty for both sides, bounds up to tell him that he scored 154 not out. 'You're wrong there,' barks Sir Geoffrey. 'I scored 176. You've given Gilliat 22 of *my* runs. I'm glad you won't be scoring in the first-class games.' Having broken the butterfly, Boycott stomps to the pavilion. The reader is left to imagine the look on the poor girl's face. And this we find in his very own book; the editor should perhaps have spared his blushes. The Authors XI's own priceless asset, Laura the Scorer, would never make such a bookkeeping boob. Mind you, none of us takes our batting so seriously as to actually count our own runs.

Boycott often laments bitterly that he never had the opportunity to see Donald Bradman bat. In his writing you can feel that frustrated need to understand just *how* a mortal could have that record average, or score 300 in a day. (On that tour in 1978/9 Boycott actually batted through a whole day of Test cricket without finding the boundary once.) Maybe we should turn to Bradman's autobiography for answers. C. L. R. James believes the key lies in a passage where the Don describes the occasion of his 100th century ('the most remarkable page in that remarkable book'). Bradman, having reached the milestone, tells how he finally allows himself the freedom to bat how he really wanted, smashing another seventy-one in forty-five minutes. It is, for Bradman, 'the most satisfying [innings] of my career'. James calls the passage 'the strangest statement I have ever read, and one to which I frequently return'. There on the page is the key to the enigma of Bradman, the greatest sportsman the world has ever known. What to make of a man who can only feel free of inhibition after twenty years of unbroken achievement and the scoring of a century of centuries?

In contrast, here's a rarely glimpsed puckish side to the relentless run machine. This is Bradman on unguarded form, writing of Gary Sobers when he played in the Don's South Australia team: 'How often have I run my fingers through his curly hair in the dressing-room and asked for a hundred, and how often has he obliged.' A delightful vignette of the two players with the strongest possible claims to be the finest the game has produced. Bradman remains, of course, the ultimate rebuttal to Australian cultural cringe: boasted *Schindler's Ark* author Thomas Keneally, 'No Australian had written *Paradise Lost*, but Bradman had made 100 before lunch at Lord's.'

If Boycott in print only occasionally lets the mask slip, his fellow Yorkshireman Fred Trueman ('t' best bloody fast bowler that ever drew breath' © F. Trueman) is more often found in confessional mode. In *Ball of Fire* (published 1976) our hero is rather candid about life off the field in those months-long tours (no WAGS permitted in those days). To remain celibate, Fred writes, was 'more than flesh and blood could bear' and his wife, an 'intelligent woman' (no less!), 'must have known I'd had a few birds'. Charming. However, when a new set of memoirs (*As It Was*) came out in 2005, time had blurred the edges of recollection. Now Fred admits to temptation but piously insists he did not stray. The reader might be forgiven for wondering what's going off out there, *Ball of Fire* indeed! If you want to get close to the real

Trueman I'd recommend sticking to John Arlott's *Fred: Portrait of a Fast Bowler*.

Dickie Bird's autobiography (published by Hodder in 1998) was the Harry Potter of cricket books – a surprise sensation. Who knew that many millions wanted to spend so much time in the company of the oddball umpire? True to type, Dickie reveals himself as a man who very much believes that cricket exists and abides for the sole benefit of the men in white coats. When England qualify for the cricket World Cup final in 1987 (Gatting's ill-fated reverse sweep and all that) Bird can't contain his disappointment that this denies him (as an English umpire) the chance to officiate in the match. Hard on the heels of the bestseller came Vol. II … followed by *Bird on Tour*, and then *Dickie Bird's Britain*. One can just imagine the Hodder money men beating a path to his editor's door and asking him to go back to the well again and again. Resurrecting the golden goose has ever been a strategy dear to publishing hearts, providing ample fodder for the favourite game of that tribe of collectors and dealers who while away the time at auctions selecting their Worst Cricket Book: Peter May's *A Game Enjoyed* usually takes the palm in the 'Dullest Title' category. But it's too easy to poke fun at modern and not so modern cricketers and their ventures into print and, as Cardus wrote, it is wise not to be too rude about cricket autobiographies as 'you never know who has written them'.

Like those novelty games (One-Arm vs One-Leg, Married vs Single, Smokers vs Non-Smokers) that turn up in the old cricket histories, the Authors XI has been mooting an interclub Fiction vs Non-Fiction game. Cricket has a chequered treatment in fiction, the myriad embarrassing failures forgotten in favour of evergreen triumphs. There are wonderful moments to be found in L. P. Hartley (a splendid evocation of that best of cricketing feelings: taking the crucial catch), in A. G. Macdonell (the 'village blacksmith' has now become a cricketing archetype) and recently in Joseph O'Neill's *Netherland* (cricket in post 9/11 New York anyone?). For so many writers it's an irresistible metaphor for some sort of Englishness. In T. H. White's irrepressibly barmy reimagining of the King Arthur myth, *The Once and Future King*, there is a gloriously anachronistic passage where Sir Lancelot is compared to an amalgam of Bradman and Woolley. A favourite is the lovely scene in Julian Barnes's *Arthur & George* where we find Arthur batting at Lord's. Inspired by the presence in the crowd of his lover, Arthur has one of those days: 'the bowlers have no secrets from him; his bat is impregnable, and scarcely registers the impact as he smacks and wheedles the ball around the field'. A perfect literary description of being 'in the zone', that much prized state when (usually as a batsman or a leg-spinner) everything seems to run in harmony. For the non-fiction complement see Mike Atherton's description of his magnus opus, the 185* at Jo'burg, or fellow Author Ed Smith's subtle analysis of the same elusive phenomenon.

****

The 'Arthur' in question was a fictionalised Arthur Conan Doyle, one of the stars of the original Authors XI. Another was P. G. Wodehouse, whose joyous cricket writing, like David Gower's cover drive, is resistant to all criticism. Today in August 2012, we are following in Wodehouse's steps at Dulwich College, all hoping, like his character Mike Jackson, to play a clean drive to put us at peace with the world, and to return to the pavilion to 'gradually swelling applause in a sort of dream'.

In Wodehouse's day, Dulwich College wickets had something of the minefield about them, and the schoolboy fast bowler duly profited. When the revived Authors turn up at the school to play the Publishers, we are met by the best-looking wicket of the season, and we're desperate to have first use of it.

Guildenstern (in Tom Stoppard's take on *Hamlet*) loses a coin toss ninety-two times in a row. Charlie 'Guildenstern' Campbell duly heads to the middle with the Publishers' captain, the ritual is performed and of course we're in the field. The sage Richie Benaud famously wrote that captaincy is 90 per cent luck and 10 per cent skill. What he failed to mention was that, in the shallow waters of friendly amateur cricket where we paddle, one key captaincy requirement is the suggestive power necessary to cajole the opposition skipper into making the 'right' decision at the toss. We fancy our chances against these Publishers. Some of them have turned down our books, and motivation is not lacking. They look a little depleted – it's a Friday and in these days of Amazon and self-publishing and vanishing bookshops, legendary long publishing lunches and sloping off to play cricket (like Mike Jackson) are things of the past. One of the opposition, horror of horrors, is sporting black trainers. If he bowls at me he will be hit for six first ball – on principle.

Our confidence is not misplaced as we make a strong start. Nick and Matthew quickly dismiss the Publishers' openers (one of them is a Blofeld, nephew to Blowers of *Test Match Special* fame). Then Nick must be hauled off following a few overs laden with lethal potential. 'Might ruin the game' is the unarticulated thought. Grazing in the covers, I feel a wave of admiration for our skilful vice-captain who, bowling beautifully, bears the decision without a shrug. In the last over of his short spell second slip was removed the very ball before an edge flies there off a perfectly pitched outswinger. It very probably wouldn't have been caught (Sebastian Faulks snaffled our lone slip catch of our season at Wormsley, and today takes a spectacular tumbling effort in the covers). Nick had been just as phlegmatic on that occasion. Such good grace is rare among the fast bowling fraternity. Fred Trueman would certainly have had something to say in similar circumstances. I captained my village Sunday side for ten years, and in a team of rampant egos we too were blessed with an opening bowler who was the model of equanimity. He reminded us all of the draught horse Boxer from *Animal Farm*.

The Publishers' captain and best batsman is Richard Beswick: studious, precise of movement and attired in an old-school buttoned cotton shirt. He has time, and looks, in Ken Barrington's phrase, like he has booked in for bed and breakfast on the flawless wicket. But Tom Holland produces a surprise lifter off a length to take his glove and Alex completes the catch; with Beswick departs the Publishers' last hope of posting a decent score (co-opted interns in the lower middle order notwithstanding). Richard Beswick is Tom's editor, and, though they've had a harmonious relationship, word does get out of an incident where Richard insisted on a rewrite of a sentence in a draft of Tom's bestselling *Rubicon*; the demanding editor deemed it rather too similar to a Tony Blair soundbite. Writers don't forget that sort of thing.

Tea is taken, and we scour the pavilion honours board for literary alumni. Wodehouse, of course, but also Raymond Chandler is there. Talk returns to the topic of cricket (and sport) in fiction, and how tricky it is to pull off. Sebastian Faulks's first novel was cricket-themed, but it failed to please him and he confesses to having destroyed the draft. As an act of literary vandalism it might not be on a par with John Murray tossing Byron's memoirs into the fire, but do not underestimate the loss to cricketing literature.

Conversely, it would have been merciful to burn a great deal of what passes for cricket poetry. Upon the refounding of the Authors, Charlie declared we would *not* be adding to the ignoble canon of cricketing verse. Thank God. It doesn't stop us quoting, though: 'Say not the struggle naught availeth', with suitable irony, has been wheeled out a few times as we have staggered towards victory or defeat (three last-ball finishes in a season of fifteen matches; those old advocates for 'brighter cricket' would be proud). What's the point of being an Authors team if you can't be a little pretentious? Cricketers will often remark on those odd green rings of grass that creep across even the most immaculate cricket square, but never before have I played in a team where, when the subject comes up, mid-on murmurs, 'Ye elves by moonlight do the sour green ringlets make, whereof the ewe bites not.' Even more than cricket prose, cricket poetry begins and ends in nostalgia. Cricket poets all wear heavily rose-tinted spectacles, ever lamenting the passing of some never-never Golden Age. Gaieties CC (whom we are to meet in their guise as Actors later in the season at Lord's) have an end-of-season ritual in which their captain recites Francis Thompson's 'At Lord's' ('For the field is full of shades …'). It's actually one of the few good cricket poems, and none the worse for the fact that it drips with nostalgia. Never has that sense of how you, the fan, really possess your favourite cricketer been better expressed (*my* Hornby, *my* Barlow). Gaieties player and President Harold Pinter once sent to Simon Gray a poem on his cricketing hero. Here it is in full:

I saw Len Hutton in his prime
Another time, another time.

Pinter waited impatiently a few days and then finally phoned up his good friend to gauge reaction. 'Oh, I haven't finished it yet, Harold,' said Gray.

I wonder whether Pinter and Gray cemented their friendship while batting together. Nothing quite matches an opening partnership for its power in turning two strangers into friends. The trust, and the sense that there are two of you against eleven of them (or thirteen, counting the umpires). The delightful Will Fiennes and I were well on that path before his sickening injury at the Valley of Rocks.

So today I'm opening with the irrepressible children's author Tony McGowan; to express the breadth and depth of his enthusiasm for cricket and the Authors XI lies beyond my powers of description. I take a single off the first ball of the innings and watch Tony, all twitches and quirks, play out the rest of the first over.

Now I'm facing literary agent Jim Gill, a competitive Scot and left-arm quick. He does *not* wear black trainers. Most uncharacteristically he serves up a long-hop on my legs. Back foot goes back and across. Wrists cocked, my beloved Newbery is at the top of its backswing in a flash. The whole leg-side is at my mercy, and I experience a rare sensation: I can feel the ball on the face of my bat, and in the moment it seems to linger there as I consider where to dispatch the inevitable four. Could this be the day when I finally experience what it is to be 'in the zone'? I then plonk the ball unerringly straight to square leg, right at the only fielder in acres of space. A half-smile of amused sympathy plays across Tristan Jones's lips as he accepts the catch.

I'm afraid the rest of the top order fares little better. The Authors are making a complete hash of our modest run chase. Thank heavens for Jon Hotten. He goes about his work at the crease calmly and prizes his wicket highly. Then skipper Charlie plays his best innings of the season, injecting vital life into our flagging effort. It takes a reaction catch from Beswick to prise him out and that costs the Publishers' captain a dislocated finger. Not a good injury for an editor. We're still short of runs. Displacement activity breaks out. Now powerless, Charlie paces the boundary as the endgame unfolds. With ten to win and two overs to go, next-but-one number eleven Tom Holland declares that, as 'a token of confidence', he will not put on his pads. This sends the skipper into a frenzy of irritation: 'Put your fucking pads on!' We lurch to victory with two balls to spare, Tom Penn and Matthew doing it in singles.

****

'Even cricketers can be extremely stupid about the value of books'
lamented that supreme technocrat of English cricket, C. B. Fry.
As befits a man who was once offered the throne of Albania, he
decides to remind us all of their value: '… they render available to
the reader a mass of knowledge … It is sheer gratuitous gain.'

Sheer gratuitous gain. Though the Authors have – just –
prevailed over the Publishers, as a precis of the value of books that
is something on which we can all agree.

*The Authors' celebrations after this game were joyous and
continued long into the night. We'd shown that we could win
without Sam making most of our runs. Having him and Nick
in the team made us competitive – without them we'd have lost
far more fixtures than we did. Which brings me to the issue of
selection, which was one of the harder aspects of organising the
Authors. We were oversubscribed for many of our games, and if
there was one match that players were desperate to be involved
in, it was at the cradle of cricket, Hambledon, where so many
of cricket's laws and peculiarities emerged.*

CRICKET AND HISTORY
Thomas Penn

Authors XI vs Hambledon CC, 12 August, Hambledon

> *If the French noblesse had been capable of playing cricket with
> their peasants, their chateaux would never have been burnt.*
> G. M. Trevelyan, *English Social History*

The word Hambledon evokes a cricketing dawn of time:
top hats and cummerbunds, and red-faced farmers
rushing in to bowl on rough pastureland, slinging
underarm deliveries furiously at each other's unpadded shins,
before retiring to devour sides of beef and barrels of ale. If, as
C. L. R. James says, cricket is 'the most complete expression of
popular life in pre-industrial England', then Hambledon Cricket
Club is the lens through which most of us see it. Hambledon's
history is one of cricket before Victorian organisation and
gentrification. This is cricket in the raw. Aristocrats gambling
breathtaking sums of money, match fixing, the decline of
traditional communities, revolts and riots: a time before the mid-
innings feast and hogsheads of port had given way to the crustless
cucumber sandwich. By the time of the French Revolution,

Hambledon's heyday was over: all the moneyed gentry who had poured funds into this very first cricketing franchise had moved away to metropolitan Lord's. The club reverted to what, over two centuries later, it remains today – a community club, but one with an extraordinary history. Hardly a wonder, then, that for the Authors CC this fixture constituted as much a pilgrimage as a cricket match.

Though I'd never been to Hambledon, its stories were for me as unforgettable as Bradman's Test batting average. I'd first read about this most historic of village clubs in the year of my cricketing epiphany, which unfortunately for me – or, to look at it another way, fortunately, given that it proved to be the mother of all inoculations against future England sporting disappointment – was 1989. It was that catastrophic Ashes summer which would trigger sixteen years of Australian dominance: the summer of 'Thatcher Out – lbw b. Alderman' and of twenty-nine England players used in a single series. In the midst of this debacle, chairman of selectors Ted Dexter increasingly resembled Chief Inspector Dreyfus from the Pink Panther films, his bewilderment culminating in his celebrated demand to the assembled press corps: 'Who can forget Malcolm Devon?'

But, untraumatised by the seemingly ever-present figures of Steve Waugh, Ian Healy and the squat, walrus-moustached David Boon (whose epic drinking session on the plane to England summed up this invincible Australian side: this, after all, was a man who could consume fifty-two cans of lager in a single flight and then walk out and demolish the England attack), I'd started to read every piece of cricketing literature I could get my hands on.

And I read about how the men of Hambledon rose out of the mists of time to take their place on the historical stage, like some kind of eighteenth-century prequel to *The Magnificent Seven*. There was Edward 'Lumpy' Stevens, by his own admission 'a bit of a smuggler', who was working quietly as gardener to the Earl of Tankerville until the earl discovered Lumpy's extraordinary ability with the ball. Lumpy, it transpired, was both accurate – Tankerville won substantial quantities of cash, betting that Lumpy could hit a feather on the pitch – and exceptionally rapid, a terrifying eighteenth-century combination of Glenn McGrath and Malcolm Marshall. The great batsman 'Silver' Billy Beldham, whose cricketing talents had hitherto gone unnoticed, was a farm labourer until, one day, he saw his employer approaching over the fields with a rich gentleman and, putting two and two together, realised that 'this was something about cricket'. David Harris was a rough diamond 'deplorably addicted to bowling full tosses' until, under the watchful eye of Richard Nyren, he was transformed into one of Hambledon's most potent bowlers. The 'stout but uncommonly active' Nyren was of course at the centre of Hambledon's cricketing life, its team captain and owner of the celebrated Bat & Ball pub, which, just a six hit from the ground, was the centre of the team's social life. A hustling entrepreneur, who in another time would probably have been more than happy to take Allen Stanford's millions no questions asked, Nyren disdained other people's reputations as readily as he inflated his own. Apparently, he liked his players to refer to him as 'The General'. His son, John, was responsible for the first work of cricketing history, a beautifully evocative – and, it must be said, somewhat dewy-eyed and myth-making – account of Hambledon's glory days, with the Nyrens firmly at the centre of the story.

Unsurprisingly, the evening before our trip to Hambledon finds me in a night-before-Christmas kind of mood. The following morning, as we drive west out of London, the capital is in the grip of post-Olympic hangover, reliving Mo Farah's epic, eye-popping, lung-busting sprint finish in the 5,000 metres the evening before. As the city gives way to suburbs and car-boot sales, the four of us

– Charlie, ace photographer Ngayu, Sam, and me – discuss the day's prospects. Sam, the rock of the Authors' innings, had been out cheaply in our previous match, an event that had struck the dressing room temporarily dumb. He is grimly determined to make up for this aberration.

Sam, enviably, is a player who strides to the crease in the anticipation of constructing a mammoth innings. I, on the other hand, model my batting game on John Emburey, my scoring areas falling roughly in an arc between third man and long leg. At school, it quickly dawned on me that I was going to have to be a bowler. Possessed of no natural pace or ability to spin the ball, I was relieved to find a category that suited my skills down to the ground: that of the dibbly-dobbly, seam-up medium-pacer. My touchstones were the likes of Mark Ealham and Ian Austin, the cerebral Derek Pringle, with his lounge-lizard saunter to the wicket, and the helping-grannies-across-the-road run-up of late vintage Ian Botham.

This Sunday morning, we leave ourselves plenty of time for a pre-match communion with Hambledon's first, most celebrated ground at Broadhalfpenny Down, and with Richard Nyren's pub, the Bat & Ball, which sits next to the ground in mellow, red-brick permanence. There, in true eighteenth-century fashion, we fortify ourselves with a few sharpeners.

We are hardly the first team to visit in search of inspiration: seeing a bat hanging from a beam, I notice with unease that it is signed by the entire 1989 Australian side. Plastered with memorabilia – from scorecards and letters to adverts, newspaper articles and title deeds – the Bat & Ball sums up the diligence with which cricket wrote, recorded and legislated itself into history, and why cricket lovers share, with all seriousness, C. L. R. James's conviction both that cricket is a way to look at history, and that history, too, immeasurably broadens and deepens your pleasure in cricket. (It was James, of course, who described an opposing team as being so obdurate they were like the last of the Three Hundred at Thermopylae, and suggested that Test matches were a way to understand the origins of Greek tragic drama.)

Certainly cricket has the ability to reflect cultures, societies, worlds at different moments in time. One of the Hambledon Club's most notorious financial backers, the womanising John Frederick Sackville, Duke of Dorset – a 'most admirable cricket player', though 'not in possession of any brains' – was, astonishingly, appointed ambassador to France at the most explosive time in that country's history. During his six-year stint in Paris, he apparently devoted most of his energies to trying to encourage the French to take up cricket. He had just succeeded in putting together the first international touring side – for a series of matches in France – when, much to his annoyance, the tour was cancelled. It was the first ever tour to be called off for political reasons. The year was 1789.

While, as a teenager, I read and listened and watched, and tried to hone my dibbly-dobbly medium pace, it dawned on me that obsessing about cricket is in fact an entirely legitimate way of passing time – which, of course, helped to ease my conscience considerably in those moments of procrastination familiar to any cricket lover ('just one more over/one more wicket/I just want to see Pietersen get his hundred', and so on). Indeed, the eminent Tudor historian Sydney Anglo is responsible for what is probably my favourite ever piece of cricketing historiography. In an irrelevant but wonderful excursus at the start of an academic article, Anglo reminisced about his undergraduate life, when he and his fellow students would while away their hours in the college café picking fantasy historical cricket teams: 'debating the rival merits of Attila the Hun and Adolf Hitler as demon fast bowlers', identifying Louis XI – that most scheming of late medieval French monarchs – as the leg-spinner par excellence, weaving his universal web of leg-spinners and googlies, and discussing the attacking stroke play of Ivan the Terrible and Vlad the Impaler. The first name on their English Monarchs XI team sheet was 'H. Tudor', 'astute, cool in a crisis and dedicated to the accumulation of huge scores'. Anglo, naturally, saw this as a perfectly valid historical exercise: 'Our calculation of a king's batting or bowling averages,' he concluded, 'was really not so very much less sophisticated than a historian's character sketch.'

I entirely agree. If you consider the celebrated 1505 portrait of Henry VII, it's easy to detect a touch of the Steve Waugh about him. He'd never be particularly good to watch – I see him as a nudger and nurdler, good off his legs, with perhaps a rasping square cut – but there would be something utterly compelling about the sheer bloody-mindedness of it all. He'd never give it away. Unflinching and narrow-eyed, you wouldn't tell from his expression whether he'd hit his previous ball for four or had been dropped at slip. Bowlers, wondering how many times he'd played and missed, would look up at the scoreboard and be astonished to find he was already thirty not out. To coin a Graham Gooch-ism, Henry VII would be the English king most likely to 'make it a daddy'.

As we lunch outside at the Bat & Ball, the Broadhalfpenny Down air is clearly working its spell on my fellow authors. Captain Charlie seems to resemble even more strongly than usual a seventeenth-century cavalier; Tom Holland, meanwhile, addresses his ploughman's like a Roman senator in his *triclinium*. But it is our glowering fast bowler Matthew Parker who appears to be most in his natural habitat. As he negotiates several ales and what he describes as a 'moob' of pâté, it strikes me that here is a reincarnation of the hard-living cricketer 'Long Robin', who liked to go to Smithfield's Bartholomew Fair and eat black puddings 'for the humour of the thing'.

After lunch, we head over to Hambledon's 'new' ground at Ridge Meadow. It's immediately clear why, sometime in the early nineteenth century, Hambledon's cricketers chose this spot. Ridge Meadow is idyllic. The ground, fast-draining chalk land, is like an upturned dish, sloping gently away on all sides to the surrounding fields. Outside the pavilion, regulars are nursing the first pints of the afternoon. On the outfield, our opponents are warming up, flinging thirty-yard throws into the wicketkeeper with casual ease. This is supposed to be Hambledon's Sunday side, including, explains the club captain Mark Le Clerq with a smile, 'a few youngsters'. This, however, is a club with three senior XIs, nine junior XIs and which provides a steady drip-feed of talent to Hampshire: the 'youngsters' are clearly quite good.

As we stroll out to the middle, I exchange thoughts with Nick Hogg. Nick also tolerates my excitable disquisitions on weather conditions. Today, it's overcast and muggy; the pitch, we discover, is slow and low. Ideal, in other words, for medium-pacers like me.

We're bowling first and Charlie, much to my surprise, gives me the new ball. Matthew Parker takes the first over, muttering irascibly to himself; down at fine leg, I watch the batsmen, all high elbows and exaggerated, Robin Smith-esque leaves outside off-stump. Then that moment of anticipation at the top of my run-up. My first ball, full of a length, shapes gently away outside off-stump. Perfect. Scoring is difficult, and the overs and dot balls tick by. At the other end Matthew steams furiously in: stumps clatter and the first wicket falls. Ambitiously, I bowl a short ball, trying to push the batsman back on to his stumps: he rocks back and deposits it over square leg. But the cloud cover and movement are still there. I turn the ball ninety degrees, holding it across the seam. Now, the batsman plays for non-existent swing: the ball thuds into his pads. The umpire raises his finger, the batsman – he must be less than half my age – disappears and the Authors converge in a flurry of high fives.

Nick replaces me: he's yards faster and the cricket increases in intensity, batsmen hurried into shots. Wickets continue to fall at regular intervals, but Hambledon's other opening batsman – another teenager – is still there, accumulating quietly. The clouds break up and the atmosphere clears; sunlight floods the ground. A partnership builds and the momentum, imperceptibly, shifts. The infield retreats. Towards the end of the innings Charlie brings me back on to bowl.

These are precisely the moments when bowlers of my kind are exposed: the early movement has disappeared and two well-set batsmen are hitting hard and running hard. And so it proves: after a chastening couple of overs I retreat to long-on. The innings comes to an end in a miasma of dropped catches, missed run-outs and sloppy fielding. Hambledon's opener, Rhidian Chapman, is left high and dry on a superb ninety-nine not out. A hundred and seventy-eight to win, off thirty-five overs: not straightforward, but gettable. Crucially, since we have bowled first, Hambledon's excellent hospitality can now be enjoyed to the full.

As tea is taken and pints are pulled, I examine a replica scorecard hanging in the pavilion. It details a match between Hambledon and All England, played at Hambledon in June 1777. In response to England's 166 all out, Hambledon made 403, with their left-hander James Aylward making 167, then the highest ever first-class score. Aylward, bizarrely, came in at number ten. Pointing out this curiosity to one of the Hambledon team, I'm soon put straight. Aylward, in fact, was a top-order batter – but in terms of social status, he came tenth out of eleven. Scorecards, in the eighteenth century, reflected how posh you were rather than the batting order. The Duke of Dorset, needless to say, was listed first on the scorecard. He was bowled, for nought.

Tea over, I wander back into the sun. As the Authors' innings gets underway, I fall into conversation with Robert 'Topsy' Turner, who – statistically at any rate – must count as Hambledon's greatest cricketer. Topsy, who only retired from the game a couple of years ago, started playing for the club when he was eleven; he's now in his mid-seventies. I catch him contemplating a chance encounter. Earlier that day a spectator at the ground, introducing himself to Topsy, said that he remembered him as a young boy. The spectator, an evacuee during the war, had worked for Topsy's father. But he had then left Hambledon and had not returned until this afternoon, almost seven decades later.

This man who had emerged out of Topsy's past had missed his extraordinary cricketing career. A bricklayer by trade, Topsy has forearms like tree trunks. When his figures were last properly totted up, he had scored over 27,000 runs and taken 3,000 wickets – and that was thirty years ago. Did he ever play County cricket, I asked him? 'I biked to Southampton for trials with Hampshire once, when I was sixteen, but lost my way and missed them. They never asked me back.'

Topsy, though, is clearly treasured by Hambledon. The club, as Le Clerq explains, remains at the heart of the local community. Many of its talented youngsters end up trialling – or, like Topsy's son Ian, playing – for Hampshire. Maintaining this kind of operation doesn't come cheap. And, says Le Clerq, gesturing at the advertising hoardings that pepper the ground, the club doesn't receive income from the ECB or from the County: financially, it is entirely dependent upon its own efforts at fundraising and the dedicated commitment of its members.

Out in the middle, the Authors' innings is progressing laboriously. Hambledon have opened with two spinners, and two more spinners have now come on to replace them. Sam is grafting hard. At the other end Charlie, more accustomed to his role as a middle-order buccaneer, lives by the sword – or, rather, his prized Laver & Wood bat – and ends up perishing by it, too. A catch reminiscent of the sixteen-year-old Sachin Tendulkar's astonishing effort at Lord's in 1990 does for James Holland after a stylish cameo, and the chase then settles into attrition. On the pavilion steps, Authorial banter gives way to anxious muttering about run rates and the occasional frantic shout of encouragement. All the while, Sam is a picture of concentration, working singles into gaps and clubbing the occasional boundary, acknowledging warm applause for his fifty with a perfunctory wave of the bat. Later, a shackle-breaking six moves him into the nineties, and then a single brings up the Authors' first century. It's an innings that surely would have elicited a thin smile from Henry VII.

Next ball, Sam is caught in the deep, prompting general groans and head clutching. As afternoon shades into evening – one of *those* evenings, in fact, like something out of a Sir Henry Newbolt poem – Hambledon's spinners continue to wheel away, and Tony McGowan and Jon Hotten flicker to and fro, Francis Thompson-style, until Jon is out, and we still need six off the last over. The first five balls yield five runs and, remarkably and satisfyingly, Nick Hogg biffs the last ball for the single we need to win.

Hambledon is a club acutely aware of its own history – but, more importantly, a forward-looking club with a deep sense of local community. And this, of course, is what kept it going through the lean years. Back in the eighteenth century, Hambledon's glory days depended on patronage, and on the huge quantities of cash being poured into the club by aristocrats and promoters. When the money dried up, the superstars and franchises left; so, too, did the massive audiences. By the mid-1790s the club was a shadow of its former self, forlorn and moribund. But, of course, Hambledon was never just a franchise. When the toffs and businessmen relocated to London and the MCC, the club kept going, its regulars turning up faithfully to meetings, as they continue to do two centuries on.

Those meetings, however, continued to attract some unexpected guests. In late August 1796, the clubhouse was rather fuller than it had been for some time. And among the attendees minuted was one 'Mr Thomas Paine, author of The Rights of Man'. Maybe this was some kind of joke – these were, after all, the years of French-inspired radicalism. Or was England's most celebrated revolutionary writer indeed in Hambledon? We know he was at Versailles on 13 August, before disappearing, unaccountably, for around three weeks. Just maybe, in the course of a clandestine mission to England, Tom Paine had pencilled in a day at the cricket.

With three wins on the trot, we approached our game at Lord's with confidence. Though Sam sounded a note of caution. He had extensive knowledge of our opponents, the Gaieties – who numbered Harold Pinter, Tom Stoppard and Sam Mendes among their luminaries – and he thought they'd be a lot stronger than us. But we've got Ed Smith, I said. Which was true. But the secret to fielding a former England player at our level of cricket is to turn up with him on the day, having given your opponents no previous warning. The Gaieties were forewarned and so came with their strongest side. We had a good crowd coming to see us, though sadly Lord's would not relent from their doggist stance, and allow our mascot, Arthur, to come and support us. This, more than anything, proved crucial. He had seen us to victory at Shepperton and against the Publishers. He was our totem and it would be difficult without him.

Lord's was, of course, the venue for the traditional match between the original Authors and the Actors and so we decided this chapter would focus on sport and stage and Dan Stevens and Ed Smith would contribute essays on the relationship between the two. This match was the undoubted highlight of our season, and the one that everyone wanted to play in. I had even had a few emails from complete strangers declaring their availability for selection. But it was hard enough finding places for our own squad. Alex Preston couldn't play and so James Holland offered to keep wicket in his stead. And Tony McGowan nobly offered to umpire on the day, allowing Ed to slot in at the top of the order with Sam.

It can't be easy for a former professional player at this level, let alone one with thirty-four first-class centuries to his name. You're expected to win matches single-handedly but with great charm and insouciance. Make a century and you've done what's expected of you. God help you if you're out for a duck. Many professional players prefer to give up playing entirely, rather than step down to this bastardised version of the game. Thankfully, Ed hasn't and his presence in the side added more than runs to our team. That day we all had a feeling of stepping up a level in so many ways. Not only were we playing at Lord's, but the crowd included journalists and commentators as well as friends and family. Coming off the pitch, we would be greeted by John Wilson and his BBC Front Row crew. Ed may be used to this – we weren't and delighted in it.

SPORT AND STAGE
Ed Smith

Authors XI vs Gaieties CC, 22 August, Lord's

D.H. Lawrence was not a noted sports writer, but one of his aphorisms, in *Studies in Classic American Literature*, captures a central truth about sport. 'An artist is usually a damned liar,' he argued, 'but his art, if it be art, will tell you the truth.'

Where is the sport here? Change the word artist for the word sportsman: 'A sportsman is usually a damned liar, but his sport, if it is real sport, will tell you the truth.' That sentence celebrates the best strands of sport, while skewering the worst.

In what way is a sportsman a liar? We should not blame them for their untruths. Evading the truth is now an all-consuming part of their job. Because sportsmen are called upon to lie all the time – on television, in interviews, even in their own thoughts – they have had to become good at it. Sportsmen are an adaptive bunch, quick learners, and they've learned to say things that appease the media, while trying to protect their true feelings from the spotlight.

A sportsman, like the artist, seeks authenticity. Being forced to analyse his work in public makes that search for authenticity much harder. Imagine asking a novelist: 'What emotional response are you trying to create in the novel you are writing? Tell us what the reader is supposed to feel.' It would negate the point of writing the book. 'If I could say it in words,' as Edward Hopper said, 'there would be no reason to paint.'

The same applies to sport – especially cricket. Cricket is not all about the execution of a pre-arranged plan. There must always be room for instinctiveness, space for your true voice to emerge. Being able precisely and truthfully to answer the question, 'How will you approach the game tomorrow?' is not always a sign of strength or preparedness. It can be a symptom of fear and narrowness. No sport can ever be turned into a perfectly predictable science, least of all cricket, with its subtle rhythms and subplots.

Before a vital County match, I remember sitting in the hotel foyer reading the paper, collecting my thoughts. The coach wandered over. 'How are you planning to play Shane Warne today?' he said, apropos of nothing. Did he want a manifesto, now, just after breakfast? 'As well as I can,' I replied. There is a lot I could have said about how I planned – or hoped – to play Warne. But given that it was far too late to develop new techniques before the match (it would have been difficult to learn a new sweep shot on the team bus), where was the advantage in turning my plan – or, better expressed, my set of intuitive responses – into a public document?

The sporting cliché has evolved for a very good reason. It is a safer, politer way of saying: 'None of your fucking business.' Faced with either intrusive or inane questions, the sane person retreats into the safety of half-truths and evasions.

If you haven't lost your authenticity before the match, there is always an opportunity to confuse yourself retrospectively. Thanks to the post-match interview – often conducted seconds after the final bell – sport has been turned into emotional pornography. 'I know you've just lost your father, so how did it feel to be walking up the eighteenth fairway needing just a par to win the Open Championship?' *The Times* sportswriter Simon Barnes – tired of hearing sportsmen fumble to describe what they feel – has suggested they reply more forcefully: 'Sorry, I'm a sportsman – I do not try to understand my feelings. We have a profession for that skill. It's called poetry. Ask one of that lot.'

And yet what truths are revealed on the pitch! When Cathy Freeman, the Australian Aboriginal athlete, stood on the starting line of the 400 metres Olympic final in Sydney in 2000, she not only carried the hopes of a nation, she embodied them. Australia is a young, optimistic country with little to be ashamed about, but its treatment of Aboriginals is Australia's original sin. That sense of guilt lent a deeper dimension to Australia's yearning for Freeman to win Olympic gold. She did. Immediately afterwards, overcome by the achievement and the pressure she had endured, Freeman sank to the track, apparently involuntarily anchored to the ground. In victory, yes; in exhaustion, certainly. But beneath those conventional emotions, surely, lay a far deeper sense of relief and achievement – about race, about how a nation can change and grow up. All this was captured on her face and in her body as she lay on the track – both spent and triumphant. Then someone shoved a microphone in her face. 'How does it feel, Cathy?' Who was revealing the truth and who obscuring it?

We see the same disconnect between real images and inadequate words in the most dazzling sport today: tennis. Ever since the rivalry of Rafael Nadal and Roger Federer first made us gasp, we have witnessed a sport shooting off into the outer stratosphere of brilliance.

Modern tennis players have become superbly gracious, partly in response to the media demands made on them. But a part of me wants to scream at the television when they are asked to give just a little bit more, when they have already given more than we could have possibly expected.

I was courtside in Melbourne when Novak Djokovic defeated Rafael Nadal over seven hours in February 2012. Both men had trouble breathing in the final set, even standing. And yet when the match finally ended, they had to stand for another thirty minutes on the court, trying to find words to describe superhuman deeds. Halfway through the presentation ceremony – it was now past 1 a.m. – someone finally noticed that the two athletes were having difficulty standing up. Two chairs were scurried to the centre of the court. But still the words went on, each one chipping away at the perfection of the sport we had just watched. Enough: no more half-truths in words! We have seen so many real truths in action!

So sport has evolved in two apparently contradictory ways. Thanks to superb television footage, we can see what really happened with greater clarity. And yet due to the explosion of the puff industry that now surrounds modern athletes, it can be harder than ever to know what is really going on. Lawrence's aphorism works perfectly on both levels. The truths revealed on the pitch: exalted. The banalities demanded at press conference: dismissed.

As Matthew Arnold wrote in this untitled poem:

> Below the surface-stream, shallow and light,
> Of what we say we feel – below the stream,
> As light, of what we think we feel – there flows
> With noiseless current strong, obscure and deep,
> The central stream of what we feel indeed.

One day, I hope, we will accept that sportsmen do not always know what they feel. And that their naivety is part of their magic.

Sport and the arts are entangled in another dimension. The word 'player', so naturally applied to sportsmen today, in fact derives from the stage. When you went to see the 'players' in

Elizabethan England, you were going to the playhouse, not the tennis court. The two meanings of 'player' – an actor or a sportsman – evolved alongside each other.

I think the sportsman and the actor share more than just a common linguistic heritage. Sportsmen are players in the other sense of the word, too. They take to the stage, they inhabit a role.

When I talk with performers – whether they are actors, singers, musicians or sportsmen – I notice shared characteristics. In 2004, I made a series for Radio 3 exploring the parallels between the lives of sportsmen and musicians. Craig Ogden, the classical guitarist, told me: 'Acting, music, cricket – the final vocational choice was partly just chance. If I hadn't become a musician, I'm sure I would have done something else that put me on a stage in front of an audience.' The activity is different – the pitch, the podium, the orchestra – but the stage is universal.

Yes, champion sportsmen are different when they take to the stage. They take on a new energy and confidence. And yet, crucially, they remain true to themselves. They do not lose their authenticity. They speak with their own voice.

Practice, preparation and discipline have been the hallmarks of professional sport. And they have made sportsmen fitter, stronger, faster and more relentless. The next generation will continue to inch forward physically. But gaining an edge through physical training becomes harder as the human body nears the point of optimality. Racehorses stopped getting faster in the 1950s. One day it will happen to humans.

There is a paradox here. Even as we push at the outer wall of the science of physiology, we remain pleasingly distant from mastering the psychological art of performance.

Here is a heretical thought. The future of sport will be defined more by the ability to find your true voice than by the business of perfecting your body. When all bodies are optimised, then the playing field is level once again – and the difference will inevitably lie elsewhere.

We will never reach – or even discern – the outer wall of inspiration. And it will always retain an element of mystery. 'If the word "inspiration" is to have any meaning,' wrote T. S. Eliot, 'it must mean that the speaker or writer is uttering something which he does not wholly understand – or which he may even misinterpret when the inspiration has departed from him.' After all, 'inspiration' derives linguistically from the concept of breath – once breathed out, it has gone for ever.

A sportsman cannot choose to become inspired. He can only allow himself to be inspired – exactly like the artist. As the literary critic Christopher Ricks put it: 'An artist is someone more than usually blessed with a cooperative subconscious, more than usually able to effect things with the help of instincts and intuitions of which he is not necessarily conscious. Like the great athlete, the great artist is at once highly trained and deeply instinctual.'

What is a 'cooperative subconscious'? Put more simply: finding your voice.

Finding one's voice has not, on the whole, been an issue for the Authors this year. We crowded round John Wilson, delighted at the thought of being on Front Row, *and eager to tell him about our season. Asked why the Authors had re-formed, Tom Holland stated that London needed a major sporting event this summer, before regaling listeners with tales of his six at Eton. A few rows back sat Daniel Norcross and Katie Walker, who present* Test Match Sofa. *Two days later, during a rain-interrupted ODI, they would talk through our match, to the slight bewilderment of their listeners, gently questioning some of my decisions.*

My first decision was to call heads, wrongly once again, and the Gaieties put us in. Sam and Ed strode out to bat, like the Authors' opening pair had over a century before. Sam, with some of the awe Wodehouse must have felt for Conan Doyle, asked Ed if he'd like to take the first ball. Ed's reply, 'Could you, so I can have a look at the bowling?', now ranks as Sam's fondest cricketing memory. These two got us off to a tremendous start, racing to fifty in the first eight overs. The pitch was true, the boundaries were short and it seemed to be a wonderful day for batting. I began to have visions that we might pass 250 for the first time this season.

I even felt twinges of guilt looking at our opposition who had no former international player in their ranks. But when the opening bowlers dismissed first Ed and then Sam, my complacency faltered. By this stage Amol and James Holland were in and brought some stability to our innings but when four wickets fell in quick succession, we looked to be in trouble.

Thankfully, Amol was in excellent form and he and I put on sixty-eight runs for the seventh wicket. It's a partnership that makes me happy just writing about it. Life doesn't get much better than to find oneself batting at Lord's, with the most ebullient batting partner imaginable. But it couldn't last. When Hugo Thurston, the opposition skipper, brought himself on to bowl, my eyes lit up after his first ball. There's a lot to be said for either bowling your best ball or your worst ball first at our level of cricket. Either will produce results. This one was the loopiest, gentlest off-break and it left me entirely unprepared for what followed, flatter, faster and turning. My subconscious had decided that I should go on the attack against one of their best bowlers and I was duly bowled by an excellent delivery.

This brought in Peter Frankopan who played the most thunderous innings of the season. He may have forgotten how to bowl since he played for Croatia, but he hit two huge sixes in his unbeaten thirty, taking us past 200. Tom had broken off his interview with Front Row *to get a first-baller. And that was that, as we were all out for 219. This was our second highest total of the season but it was never going to be enough against a side as strong as the Gaieties. We bowled well enough but we were missing Waheed's guile and variety and Matthew's aggression. Hugo Thurston and his brother put on ninety-nine for the third wicket, as the Gaieties eased past our total. Ed bowled well at the end, and set the field with an authority that I could never match, but it was not enough. It was a memorable day, though, and we all have Ngayu's spectacular photos with which to remember it. In particular there's one of Amol batting, his mouth open, as if in awe of the stroke he'd just played.*

The Authors may have been photographed but we've yet to be filmed. The exception to this is Dan Stevens. Not only has he greatly enhanced the Authors' appeal to the female population (Ngayu's photos received tens of thousands of hits after Dan's debut at Shepperton), but he turned out for the Downton Abbey *side over the summer, and this was the climax of the third series. He is also the only one of us to have played cricket in the period costume of the original Authors.*

EDWARDIAN CRICKET AND
DOWNTON ABBEY
Dan Stevens

I can't sing, but I know how to, which is quite different.

Noël Coward

I'm still not entirely sure where this chapter fits in, but then I'm still not entirely sure where *I* fit into the team. An actor among authors? Admitted on a technicality as much as anything, certainly not on merit; the fact that I have been known to put pen to paper – perhaps more often than bat to ball – seems to have qualified me. Having relinquished most, if not all, sport as an adult, cricket is one of those few activities that – especially as an actor – one can take up again after a lengthy leave of absence without too much exclamation of 'Not the face!', so long as you are wearing a helmet. More than, say, rugby. In fact, the 'can do', or 'can probably do', attitude of an actor lends itself quite well to the motley, have-a-go nature of a team like the Authors XI. I can ride a horse. I can play the violin.[1] I can't play cricket, but I know how to, which is quite different.

---

1 For 'can' read 'if pushed will try to' or 'will claim I can in an audition'.

What doesn't lend itself quite so well to a delightful, leisurely season of cricket such as that lined up for the Authors is the persistently unpredictable schedule of an actor. It truly is a pain when work gets in the way of cricket. A film set can be a great place to tune into the Test, whiling away the hours between takes, especially when one of your fellow actors is cricket-mad chairman of Hampstead CC Jim Carter, aka Carson the Butler. However, very little can ease the frustration of knowing that on a gloriously sunny day, while you are trussed up in white tie, repeatedly serving yourself stale peas in a dark and stuffy dining room at Highclere Castle, the Authors are frolicking at one of the more attractive grounds in the country, their progress barely trackable on Twitter. Why on earth don't these stately homes have wi-fi?

It was on one such interminable afternoon, sweltering into three-piece tweed, that I arrived on to the set of *Downton Abbey* to discover Carson bristling with excitement, those famous eyebrows positively quivering with delight:

'Have you heard the news?' the authoritarian basso whispered with a muffled boom.

On a day like that, when the end of play seems so far away, anything can lighten the mood; a new packet of biscuits by the tea table can seem like the greatest of victories. Especially for Carson, whose main job 'upstairs' is to stand to the side and observe proceedings, occasionally topping up the Sauternes, the thirst for jollity is great.

'Cricket match. Episode eight.' He mouthed the words so enthusiastically and yet so hushedly he could barely contain them. As the series have progressed plot secrecy has heightened to the extent that such information arrives and spreads with a frisson of forbidden pleasure. After all, at that point we were only halfway through filming episode six. To have knowledge of anything two episodes ahead felt unnatural – almost illegal.

I am speechless. This is brilliant. Every series contains one or two 'community scenes', be it a garden party, flower show, picnic or concert, which facilitates most of the principal cast being in one location for a grand '*Downton* display', multiple exchanges and plot strand-tying. This is perfect; the gents in the middle, the ladies sipping tea, gossiping at the boundary, class divides bridged. Highclere Castle already boasts a very fine cricket ground, in existence since the mid-nineteenth century, enclosed by ancient woodland with a beautiful, old pavilion, its wooden floors wonderfully gnarled and honed by a century and a half of woodworm and aristocratic spikes.

For weeks this is all we know and conversation churns as to who will play, what they will score, how they will be out. Imaginary batting orders are cast and mock shots played out among the men. Eventually a top-secret script arrives, high-waisted whites are fitted and every day the 'Promised Land' of the cricket match, to be shot in July, looms ever nearer. As the set-piece culmination of the main body of the third series it will be an epic undertaking; several pages of dialogue involving almost all the cast and specially hired camera cranes; multiple scenes and scenarios woven together and resolved, and all the while a glorious cricket match at its centre. The weather forecast looks to conspire against us, however, and one of the wettest, greyest Julys on record besets the run-up. Tensions are high.

As if proof were needed that God loves *Downton*, but perhaps more so that God loves cricket, the appointed days arrive and turn into three of the only days of sunshine England has seen in many months. Marquees are erected around the ground, sheltering the dames of Downton, resplendent in their fine cream lace and hats. The boys emerge in their whites and cloth caps, ancient pads and brown sausage-fingered gloves. As soon as the props department releases the antique stained bats and balls, the realisation dawns that we have before us three whole days of this: 'knocking about' at work. When padded up I take to the middle at any opportunity, whereupon an entire team of 'extras' bowl at me and field – and there is no getting out; the most idyllic nets session imaginable. Neil Burns, the former Leicestershire and Somerset wicketkeeper/ batsman, is on hand as our 'period style' coach, encouraging a more upright, W. G. Grace-style address, with wider hand positioning on the bat, which, while different from the modern technique, invariably improves my batting.

Of course, there is serious work to be done; the script dictates that my character, Matthew Crawley, opens the batting with a perfect cover drive. No pressure then. Burns explains the history of the community match and the different styles that would make up an estate's team. The gentlemen would generally favour the off-side, seen to be the more upstanding, attractive and 'correct' side to play the ball. However, it was recognised that this aesthetically pleasing style of play was not always conducive to a high enough run rate to beat the locals and hence the big-hitting, burly farmhands were recruited, unashamed to tonk the ball leg-side for considerably more. Far from being an elitist sport, cricket became a leveller in these instances and great respect and honour could be earned by saving the 'Earl's Eleven' with an ugly yet glorious six lodged in a 500-year-old oak tree.

Accuracy has never been a virtue of dramatised cricket. Writers seem so fond of that strange cricketing word 'Howzat!', a great sporting neologism that's tricky to weave in to any other situation. Whether Molesley's off-peg is knocked back, or the umpire raises his finger as those poles leave the ground, even if the climax of the sequence demands a wicket is taken by a catch (when, of course, the appeal would be redundant), the script will almost invariably call for a victorious vocalisation of the event. And if it's in the script, so be it. In television one would sooner bend the rules of cricket than tamper with the writer's scene: it's just not cricket. Even though it is.

As a dramatic device the match serves the show well; all manner of scenes are played out on the boundary. As in any real team the game at Downton allows each of the characters to shine through their style at the crease: the Irishman Branson reluctant, unorthodox but ultimately victorious; 'nasty' Thomas curiously brilliant and high-scoring; Molesley talking a good game but a bag of nerves beneath. And Matthew Crawley? Noble, technically elegant but dismissed for fourteen by those simple letters: lbw. He might have mastered the cover drive but not how to drive: RIP. Thank God they play cricket in heaven.

I have high hopes that the Authors will be filmed one day but we will never be able to match the on- and off-field dramas of Downton Abbey. *And despite what Tony might claim, the class tensions do not burn quite as fiercely.*

After Lord's, we were due to play a team of financiers. But they proved elusive. No bank would put out a team to face us, no doubt fearing another wave of public hatred, as they played this supposedly elitist sport. So instead we had an enjoyable Twenty20 match in Dulwich against a motley crew of friends and friends of friends, a couple of whom had once worked in the City. Tom Holland took time from the furore surrounding his programme, Islam: The Untold Story, *to play for us. Channel 4 had received over a thousand complaints following transmission and Tom composed his thoughtful and brave response to his critics on his iPad in the field. His fielding — never his strongest suit — suffered further but his bowling was manful and he took three wickets. Sam had torn his calf and injured his shoulder, and in his absence Joe Craig made a fine fifty but the Authors succumbed in a tense match. By this stage of the season, only the diehards (led by Jon and Tony) were playing in every match, as it became harder and harder to put a team out. Sam defied medical advice to take his place at the head of the batting order and in the slips. We headed north to the club where Nick had learned the game.*

CRICKET AND HOME
Nicholas Hogg

Authors XI vs Barkby United CC, 27 August, Barkby

> *There was an air raid. We opened the door and our garden,*
> *with this large lilac tree, was alight all along the back wall.*
> *We were evacuated straight away. Though not before I took my*
> *cricket bat.*
>
> Harold Pinter

My father knows something about cricket, bats and obsession.

Halfway down the wicket, darting for a quick single in the regional final of the 1980 National Village Cup, he was sent back. One set of spikes stuck, and the other slid. He went down as if a sniper had picked him off from long-on. A calm, mild-mannered social worker during the week, the only time I've ever heard him swear is in whites. He didn't say 'Fiddlesticks' when his ankle cracked and the swooping fielder whipped off the bails.

Thankfully, the opposition was a colliery club, one of many in that part of the Midlands, and a member of the opposition was the pit medic. He took one look at my father's ankle and excitedly called for a stretcher, forgetting that the First Aid facilities were no more advanced than a bucket and sponge. However, several enterprising players cleared the tea table and jogged it on to the pitch.

Still, the medic wasn't happy about moving his patient without setting the joint. It looked like a nasty break, and my father should really stay on the wicket until the paramedics arrived.

Then the skipper reminded the medic this was a knockout game, that they were winning and that the grand final would be played at Lord's. Using two bats and several yards of tape, the medic hastily bound my father's leg into a willow cast. Rolled on to the tea table by the helpful opposition, he was hoisted from the game.

Meanwhile, the incoming batsman was nearly timed out. He couldn't find his bat – it was firmly attached to my father's leg, which was now speeding away in the ambulance.

After arriving at casualty and hearing the doctor was a keen cricketer, my father hoped for sympathy. The doctor tutted at the run-out, and then cut away the tape and removed the bats.

Now, as any cricketer understands – and perhaps *only* a cricketer understands – once an unfamiliar blade is lifted the overriding instinct is to feel the pick-up and play a couple of air shots. Prior to examining the severity of my father's fracture, the doctor examined the Gunn & Moore splints. And then swished, no doubt picturing his middled drives skittering along the corridor and ricocheting off the theatre door.

At the very start of the Authors' season, waiting for the resident bat maker in the GM factory reception, I urged my father not to tell him about my first bat – a beaten-up Cannon he sawed the end off to sufficiently lighten for the swing of a ten-year-old. The effect was a long handle and a short blade, so it's no surprise that I'm a player who likes to hit. A forward defensive on a garden wicket with more handle than face was hardly the best choice of shot, and, once my parents divorced, my coaching sessions were cut down to the odd weekend that didn't rain. Any technique demonstrated on a Saturday afternoon was forgotten by Monday morning.

The headmaster of Merton County Primary School was an angry Welshman. If not bellowing down the hallways, he was coaching us to spin-pass footballs like scrum-halves – which turned out to be no bad thing when I took up rugby to fill in the gaps between cricket seasons – and the closest we ever got to a game of cricket was rounders. Until an old set of stumps, bails and pads found its way from the Nottinghamshire Social Services kitbag into my hands. Every day I lugged the entire set across the estate so that break times could be spent impersonating Ian Botham.

After school I carried the stumps down to the park, and with a core of cricket-mad friends played until the light faded. Or until the big lads strutted over and swung like hunters clubbing a baby seal. Fooling a local thug with a googly was suicide. The trick was to serve up a pie they could smash towards the gang of girls drinking Scandia Green on the swings. Thankfully, they were more impressed with how many backspins John Hillman could do than how far he could swat a waist-high full toss.

When the long summer days shortened into winter nights, we needed a new ground. Twelve years before the first official floodlit match in England, a game between Warwickshire and Somerset in 1997, the Syston Winter Streetlight Series was played every night beneath yellow bulbs behind Kwik Save. Except for noxious fumes emanating from the plastics factory, or a passing copper catching us on the fragile roofing fetching down a six-and-out, play continued until bedtime curfews, lost balls or vicious fights between the Cartwright brothers about lbws.

All this practice, combined with the DNA of my cricketing father and the hand-eye coordination of a mother who played County tennis, meant I was surely starting secondary school as the best player in the year.

The Prodigy

On a bright and crisp February afternoon, the Authors gathered outside the gleaming Edgbaston stands for an inaugural, pre-season coaching session. Naturally, the training facilities of the national side befit a team of middle-aged writers. Although it had been nearly twenty years since I'd last seen our coach, I've never forgotten the first time I bowled at him.

It was in my first week at Roundhill Community College, a crumbling Victorian state school, sited between a gargantuan landfill and the Walkers Crisps factory, that I saw him. He was taking guard against the sports hall with an aluminium pipe for a bat. And I was actually walking through the playground and not running from the barbarian hordes of the upper years. Hunting Season had begun, a tradition whereby the older, hairy man-boys chased down the pre-pubescent fledglings and kicked the shit out of them. The teachers' strikes meant policing of breaktimes was assigned to a pair of arthritic dinner ladies who bunkered down in the tuck shop. This was a glimpse of the post-apocalypse, and standing around to watch a kid face an incoming tennis ball was a risky endeavour. Then he effortlessly clipped one over the swimming-pool roof, and I loosened up.

I was about to bowl my first delivery to Darren Maddy, future Leicestershire, Warwickshire and England player, and I tore in with all my eleven-year-old might.

I can still see the ball now, forever gaining height over the Science Labs.

For the next five years, until Maddy ditched his A-levels to sign a full-time contract with Leicestershire, I was the second best cricketer in school. From that first straight six, I had no doubt that he'd play for England. He lived, breathed and ate cricket. He loved cricket before he knew what love was. When I learned of the bet that Chris Smith collected on his brother, Robin, playing Test cricket, I asked my father to place a similar wager on Darren

Maddy. He never did. Maddy made his Test debut against New Zealand in 1999.

Part of the teacher protests included a refusal to organise extra-curricular activities, like putting together a cricket team.

Fortunately, three miles across the cornfields at the back of school, in direct contrast to the chimney stacks of Walkers Crisps and Pukka Pies, is a pretty village listed in the Domesday Book. With a cricket club. The game in Barkby was first recorded in the 1700s, and in 1850 an official team was formed by the local lord.

A perfect fixture for a visiting side of writers. Trees and history, the bucolic setting. If only the weather would make the effort the rest of us are making. All week I'm obsessively checking the forecast. I want to return to the ground where I first played, this time wearing my gleaming Authors' shirt.

In 1985, wearing tracksuit bottoms and sky-blue Pony trainers, I ran in to bowl at boys in pressed whites. Kit. Boxes, boots and thigh pads. Coffins to load their cricket paraphernalia into.

My bowling was wild, and my batting hit or miss. Peter Booth, a Yorkshire-born coach who'd recently retired from the County circuit, saw an action worth taming. He straightened my front arm, turned me side-on to the batsman and introduced me to the art of swing bowling.

Peter Booth was Mr Cricket. Spiffingly turned out in whites that could cause snow blindness, he was a stickler for correct technique. Standard punishment for slogging, not running the bat over the crease, or failing to back up at the non-striker's end, was a lap of the ground.

Despite my natural desire to hit, the forward defensive Peter Booth drilled into me is the first shot I'll play when I get to the crease today. Regardless of the ball bowled. By God, I've practised enough. Hours of bedroom forward defensives, walking to school flicking leg glances into front gardens, bowling conkers at lamp-posts.

If not playing cricket, I was following the County Champion-ship at Grace Road. One man and his dog, old ladies bundled up in tartan blankets and an immaculately dressed West Indian gent who ate a stick of Kit-Kat at every fall of wicket, made up the spectators. When the sun did shine, and the outfield glowed as if cut from the cloth of a snooker table, and maybe Gower got some runs, one could forget the dilapidated stands and rotten benches and the tatty surrounds transformed into a magical arena.

We soon realised that getting to the ground early meant we could cheekily ask batsmen if they wanted us to throw them a few down. I bowled at Phil DeFreitas and the late Wilf Slack. I have a memory of bowling at Viv Richards, but this could be fanciful imagination. He was, and still is, my batting hero. An after-dinner story goes that he was facing Glamorgan paceman Greg Thomas, and playing and missing. Thomas came down the wicket and told Richards, 'It's red and it's round and it's made of leather.'

Richards put the next delivery into the River Taff. 'You know what it looks like, you go and fetch it.'

Today, neither of the Authors' opening bats has put a ball in the Barkby brook, but it's a solid start to our innings. And, most importantly, the sky's curtains of rain have been mercifully drawn above the ground.

In my youth, days when the rain did stop play, we set up the Test Match board game and rolled a silver ball down a plastic gulley attached to a miniature bowler. To simulate a prevailing wind or increase the pace, we glued the felt outfield on to plywood and tilted accordingly. From a tabletop in a cramped kitchen I imagined that I was Malcolm Marshall or Wasim Akram, and dutifully recorded their figures in the score book. Yet, no matter how thrilling the fantasy was, imagining, or even watching cricket, has never been equal to playing.

After a few seasons of Peter Booth's coaching and nets with Maddy, I'd earned a Leicestershire Schools trial. Apart from me,

Maddy and an elegant Indian batsman – aptly named Sunil, and who I'd have numerous battles with over the following seasons – there was only one other boy not from a private school. He was also the only other one late.

We met on the bus to the ground, Wygesston Grammar School. He was wearing his whites and had an Afro like Phil Simmons. We lobbed our kitbags over the railings and broke in like vandals, getting a bollocking from the cricket master. It couldn't have done our chances any favours. Other boys had been chauffeured by parents with shiny cars, and the fathers who'd taken the day off were already petitioning for their sons' inclusion in the side.

Not that I or the young Phil Simmons needed any help. He flayed the bowling to all corners of the ground, and I took wickets in a spell where I had the ball bending like a banana, Maddy snicking one to Sunil at first slip.

Although we both got through the trial, and were invited back the following day, I was intimidated. Not by the ball, nor the future Test batsman taking guard. I was intimidated by cut-glass accents and Range Rovers, bags of kit and doting parents.

Phil Simmons Jr didn't show for the next trial. Neither did I. When I should have been running in to bowl on the manicured field of a grammar school, I played cricket on the local park.

Boys to Men

I jog to the wicket as usual, keen to be at the crease. Barkby have another Authors scalp, Jon Hotten, out spooning back a long-hop to the canny all-rounder Dave Raven.

Unless there's a flurry in the last ten overs, we're going to finish short of a defendable total. Amol walks halfway across the pitch to start his advice speech. He's full of piss and vinegar at the best of times, and following his forty-that-should-have-been-fifty at Lord's, he's in the forties again with another fluid knock.

'Plenty of runs out here, mate.'

I beg to differ. I'm about to face a bowler I once watched devastate batting line-ups.

In his pomp, Kevin Flowers was a swearing, mustachioed paceman who still recalls the season that I took three wickets on my 1st XI debut, and seven in my second game. A season in which his firebrand bowling won him a call-up to the Leicestershire Senior League County side, and also secured him league bowler of the year. Surely he'd walk away with the team honours.

Minimum qualification for the prize was ten wickets, and my rough calculation put mine at about five runs apiece. At the village hall awards dinner a fifteen-year-old pup stood up to collect the golden totem. Flowers was halfway out of his seat before he realised my name had been called and not his. From that evening on, I knew I was bowling well when his moustache twitched obscenities at me from fine leg.

Admittedly, I'm nervous taking guard against Flowers today. Now in his mid-fifties, I hope he's lost his verve. The bushy tash has been shaved off, and last time we played he couldn't bowl after cutting his toe on a Flymo blade.

But his first four balls pitch on a length outside off-stump, and either I play that Peter Booth forward defensive or miss.

'Come on, Oggy, it's not a fucking Test match.'

Thankfully, Rajan is clipping runs to all corners from the other end. I tell the young off-spinner that he's bowling at the author of *Twirlymen: The Unlikely History of Cricket's Greatest Spin Bowlers*. Excited, eyes wide at the thought of a mention in the bestselling follow-up, he flights one beautifully. And Amol lofts him on to the Beeby Road, strutting down the wicket and tapping down an imaginary tuft.

'Told you, mate. Plenty of runs.'

Not that I'm cocky. Because next on to bowl is Craig Hendry, a broad-shouldered hulk a few inches off seven feet. A fencer by trade, when not spanking sixes over the Leicestershire countryside he's swinging a sledge hammer one-handed. I've also seen his yorkers, delivered from a height that brushes the upper boughs of the oak tree, pole-axe many a batsman.

I take guard, and watch Craig lope in. He's smiling like a happy assassin. I realise I've never faced his bowling before, and that he's more than just another cricketer – as are all the Barkby veterans playing the Authors today. These are my real-life cricketing heroes, the men who bought me congratulatory beers after victories and slapped me on the back when I bowled well, who became my surrogate fathers.

On and Off the Pitch

Weeks after turning seventeen, after a night in the pub toasting another win, I was kicked out of home by my stepfather. With nothing more than my kitbag I trudged on to the park and found a spot to doss down. When I woke up cold I wore my whites over my clothes to keep warm.

I could hardly play cricket if I was on the streets, and at dawn I sought the obvious shelter. My captain's house. Until our opening batsman moved in with his girlfriend and offered me his flat, I stayed with Craig.

Twenty years after he took me into his home, I'm facing his bowling. I play down his first couple of deliveries. Cautious, respectful. A debt of gratitude owed to the man who gave me a room.

Then the third ball pitches in the magical arc, the length my father used to bowl at me while batting with the sawn-off blade. Apparently, and quite believably, unless I struck the ball out of the garden I'd throw a tantrum, and my father became adept at bowling a cow corner line and length.

Which is where Hendry puts his third delivery.

With a combined feeling of guilt and pride, I singe the ball over the sight-screen.

The winter following my ejection from home, I worked shifts in a factory and studied for my A-levels, while playing the rugby of my life and netting with the County U19s at Grace Road. One of the resident pros coaching was Chris Lewis. Lightning off a few paces, easy-going and friendly. He also bought us chips after training. Of all the able instructors, it was Chris Lewis's net we wanted to join.

In 2009, months after his failed comeback to professional cricket, when he was sentenced to thirteen years for smuggling cocaine, I blamed the game for his demise. Not necessarily the clubs, managers or administrating bodies, but cricket. The contest. Winning and losing. Belonging to a sport that can make or break a delicate ego.

Alan Butcher, Lewis's head coach at Surrey, described him as a player 'who never quite fulfilled what he wanted to do as a cricketer', and never found anything to replace it.

By the start of the following season my hair was to my shoulders, and I was nicknamed 'Sonia', after the red-headed popstrel from Liverpool. I was also dabbling in drugs that did nothing to enhance my performance. No matter how wasted I got, cricket was never far from my altered mind. An hour after dissolving my first LSD trip I was drawn to the hills and furrows of the ancient outfield, silvered in the light of a harvest moon.

My surrogate fathers warned and wagged their collective fingers. I didn't listen. After all, I was getting attention. And I was young enough to drink all night and bowl ten overs on a Saturday. So what if I got pissed and high three or four times a week? I was still playing cricket, and had even managed to win my first cap for Leicestershire U19s.

Then, on the Barkby tour to Norwich, I challenged my fellow guzzler of a dozen vodka and blacks to a chin-up contest using a Fire Exit sign as a bar. When the ceiling collapsed we escaped on to the hotel roof. By the time the police arrived I'd redecorated my room with blackcurrant cordial and chicken tikka masala, which ultimately saved me from arrest, as the baulking officers arranged to return in the morning when I was showered and conscious.

I knew something was wrong when senior players shunned me at breakfast. Then I was told of what destruction I had caused, and how my behaviour had tarnished the club's name. After begging the hotel manager not to call the police, I went outside to where the bus was waiting. My surrogate fathers had left one free seat at the very back. In complete silence I took a long walk of shame along the aisle, only to be told I'd been dropped from the side. I was sent home from the tour.

The Three-year Test

Amol holes out after reaching his half-century, possibly exhausted after all the theatrical bat-raising to celebrate his maiden fifty, before Charlie goes first ball swishing at a Hendry yorker. Next in is my old university friend Jon Gibbard. Although we've only appeared together on a full-size pitch once before, I've watched him play cricket for thousands of hours.

We met a few weeks after my dismissal from the Norwich tour, and, within days of moving into our campus dormitory, we began to demolish the kitchen.

The wicket was the cupboard door beneath the sink, and the adjoining doors first and second slip. Silly mid-on was the fearless fridge-freezer, while conventional mid-on and mid-off were patrolled by the armchairs. No swing from the TV end, but the mini basketball would grip and turn violently off the carpet tiling. With flawless bat/pad work from the MDF fielders, nifty feet and soft hands were key to a score. Lunch and tea breaks were announced by the *Neighbours* theme tune, though play could also be stopped by the non-cricketing residents invading the pitch to cook Spaghetti Hoops.

By the third year we were squatting. No deposit to lose square-cutting through a kitchen window. The long, narrow room was built for driving, and only the athletic bean bag was capable of pouching a catch. I taped a set of stumps to the lounge wall and wielded a full-size Gunn & Moore. It was the best indoor stadium of our three-year tour, and witnessed epic struggles between bat and rubber ball.

Alas, cricket, despite giving me a home when I had none, had also ruined my GCSEs and A-level grades and was now about to kick me out of university. While supposedly studying for an autumn retake I'd been twatting around positioning furniture to stem the flow of runs leaked by the useless coffee table.

I needed a degree-saving revision session. Although my muscle memory for driving and cutting was honed, the neural pathways for sitting and studying were as flabby as Gatting's midriff.

Still, I had five minutes before starting my revision, and I switched on the final day of the 1995 Johannesburg Test. Just five minutes, I resolved, then I'd hit the books.

England were batting to save the match. Barmy Army trumpeter Billy Cooper forlornly tooted the Retreat as Robin Smith and Atherton trudged to the middle. I watched five minutes. And then another five. Donald was launching Exocets, and once he got Smith I realised this was a ridiculous way to crash out of university.

I switched off the TV and opened my books, read about Freud and Jung, the collective unconscious. When I looked at the stumps taped to the wall, I pictured Atherton swaying away from a Donald bouncer. *I could hear* the ball smacking into the palm of Richardson's gloves.

Just five more minutes.

Atherton and Russell were still at the crease, Donald raging. Between balls I read and took notes.

Ball, bat, Jung.

Ball, bat, Freud.

A rhythm was building. Atherton, Russell and Hogg making a last stand, a triumvirate rearguard. Russell scuttled across the crease and defended with his buttocks. Hogg started to recall dates of studies, and Atherton even began hooking. If all three of us maintained a Zen focus, the degree could be saved.

Ball, bat, Jung.

Ball, bat, Freud.

Six hundred and forty-five minutes, 492 balls, 185 runs and several chapters later, Atherton, Russell and Hogg saluted the crowd, and Ray Illingworth described my gutsy study session as 'one of the greatest ever'.

****

My innings at Barkby today might not equal Atherton's efforts, or the epic note-taking required to achieve my Psychology Bachelor's. However, another smite off Hendry, some sharp running by Gibbard, and a cross-batted slog into the cow field off a fuming 'Who-the-fuck-coached-you-that?' Flowers, and I'm forty-nine not out.

With one ball left in the innings to make a homecoming fifty.

Have Bat, Will Travel

Naked, I lay curled in the foetal position on a bathroom floor in Mumbai. 'Travel, see the world' was the sage advice.

Go to India, see the world fall out of your arse.

I was backpacking, alone. And ill. My life-support system was the Test match, a flickering TV screen cooling the room with a mint-green outfield, and the soothing commentary of Sunil Gavaskar.

Five days later I stumbled from the hotel and headed straight for the Azad Maidan, the park where Mahatma Gandhi addressed one of the largest ever political rallies. It's also home to twenty-two cricket pitches and the wicket where a schoolboy named Sachin Tendulkar starred in a record stand of 664.

Still wobbly with fever, malnourished and dehydrated, cricket would bring me round.

The park was filled with men playing cricket, hoping the dry, brown pitches might sprinkle them with the same magic dust they'd sprinkled over the Little Master. I walked up to a game and asked if I could bowl. Rusty, I wasn't expecting to finish the over, or to be asked to play in the match, and then to bat, but the moment I pitched that first ball I transformed from a foreign tourist into a fellow cricketer.

I played on litter-strewn waste ground with bats cut from tree bark. Games by runnels of sewage with balls of tape. Players invited me to weddings and funerals. Cricket welcomed me into all castes, and I ate in grand, colonial houses, in twee stone cottages perched above tea estates, and in desperate slums.

I was supposed to be in India to write. After finding a cheap hotel by the sea in Kovalam, I took a rickshaw to the local sports shop and bought a set of stumps and bails. On a wet sand wicket smoothed by the Arabian Sea, with teams made up of chefs and porters from the cafés and restaurants lining the shore, we woke at dawn and played frenetic games in the surf. After the early morning thrash, the afternoon word count spiralled.

Ultimately, travel, romance and writing would curtail my formal cricket for over a decade. Yet I never stopped thinking about bat and ball. If stuck in an interminable play or a stifling lecture, I found myself in a spot at the edge of the stage, wondering what kind of pace I could generate off a carpeted aisle, the polished boards.

Even when I worked on an ocean-going liner I mustered up games on the tilting deck – you could slant the ball in or away from the batsman, depending on the swell – and eventually had my love for club cricket reignited in the Tokyo Indoor League, when the Japan Ladies' opening bat beautifully cover-drove my first competitive delivery in over ten years. *She loved cricket.* To play a shot of such exquisite precision she must have practised it for hours.

I'd been out of the game too long. Writing instead of batting. Reading instead of bowling.

I flew back to London and searched for a team. Aged thirty-seven, a yard of pace slower, and now as flexible as the Tin Man in the field, it was still a joy to be playing. I was simply happy to be in whites again. Then, following a rained-off game with fellow obsessive Charlie, we realised that we could combine our shared loves, cricket and writing, in a single season.

****

Now, after two novels and a decade of globe-trotting, a fifty at my home ground beckons. One run off one ball, and Gibbard knows it, backing up halfway down the track and almost overtaking Hendry's final delivery. It's blessedly straight, and I drop a bat on it and sprint in for the half-century.

Jam and Scones

I've been telling the Authors about Barkby teas all season, and the smorgasbord laid out does not disappoint. In fact, it feels like a trap. When Tony McGowan swoops for another round of cakes and chicken drumsticks, I warn him about mobility in the slips, but he taps his stomach and promises, 'There's plenty more room in there.'

Thankfully there's a delay in returning to the field, a presentation to the U11s, runners-up in the County cup. Their coach, Mark Tebbut – once praised by Muralitharan as being one of the few keepers who could read his doosra – thanks the Authors in a gracious speech, and speaks to my heart when he says that, no matter how far you travel, you never really leave Barkby.

Then we take the field, tea and scones gurgling. If the opening bat, Henry Mount, has an average equal to his waistline, we could be in trouble. But he's a victim of his aunt's famous baking, and now one of my outswingers, finely snaffled in the webbing of Charlie's gloves. Smiling, Henry tucks his bat under his arm and walks back. He knows there'll still be leftovers, and his two-ball duck comes with the consolation of clotted cream and home-made jam in the pavilion.

Unfortunately, a thriving Barkby youth policy means the whippersnappers hit sixes off length balls. The run rate steeples, and half a Victoria sponge foils Tony's efforts on a sharp chance in the slips, before Jon Gibbard strikes for the Authors. Local stalwarts Flowers and Raven make brief appearances, only for the umpire to twice raise his finger. Both lbw. And both incredulous at the decision. From what I can recall, neither of them has ever been out. Ever.

When Barkby are five down, there's brief excitement in the Authors ranks.

'We're not out of this yet, lads,' pumps Amol. 'Couple of magic balls and we're there.'

I fake optimism. I know who's in next.

Hendry walks to the wicket. His bat weighs 3lb 5oz, and I doubt he's happy about my sixes off his bowling. Goliath has risen from the grave, and this time David's feeble stones – my outswingers – are launched back over his head. I'm lucky to finish my spell with a brace.

Jon Hotten has the unenviable task of felling the titan. Scores are tied, and Barkby need one run off eleven overs to win, which might be a big ask. Craig once hit a century in twenty-six balls; we need sixty-six dot balls to save the match.

Hendry drops his mammoth bat on Jon's first delivery to finish the game, and the barbecue is lit. I've never known a loss feel more like a win. Barkby won't take a penny off us for teas or a match fee, and the welcome is extended by local farmer, Tom Pick, who grills sausages and burgers sourced from the very next field, while regaling my laughing team-mates – from both sides – and my father, with anecdotes of the infamous Norwich tour.

It feels like a party, a family reunion, presided over by that most generous of hosts, cricket.

For our last match we drove further north to Nottinghamshire. We were joined by two new recruits in Ben Falk and Ed Howker, neither of whom saw a six-hour round trip to play cricket as unusual, and Matthew brought his son, Ollie.

CRICKET AND CLASS

Anthony McGowan

Authors XI vs Kirkby Portland CC, 8 September,
Kirkby Portland

It is little I repair to the matches of the Southron folk.
Francis Thompson, 'At Lord's'

We drove through a broken landscape of scuzzy fields and the sort of light industrial estates that produce nothing useful or beautiful. The road wound through redbrick council estates, where right-to-buy gaudiness (stone cladding, gnomes, fake battlements, for all I knew, a fucking moat) was interspersed with boarded-up windows and flaking paint. Around us were spent pits, and the spoil thereof. Old men, with faces like Easter Island monoliths, stared at us without curiosity.

It was Nottinghamshire rather than Yorkshire, but still, after the manicured playing fields of Eton and Dulwich College, or the twee loveliness of the Chalke Valley, this felt – to me if not the other members of the Authors CC – like home.

The Authors had travelled north in search of class and history, and we'd found them at the ground where perhaps the greatest

fast bowler England has ever produced first plied his trade. Back
in the 1920s it was home to Nuncargate, the club for whom
young Harold Larwood first marked out his long straight run-up
– so long, in fact, that the farmer had to cut a gap in the hedge
beyond the boundary to accommodate it. You can imagine the
mocking laughter of the opposition batsmen as the frail-looking
teenager disappeared into the barley to begin his run-up. Well,
unlike Larwood's run-up, the laughter didn't last for long.

Larwood, who left school at fourteen to go down the pit,
famously became the weapon – both broadsword and rapier –
with which the Australians were overcome in the Bodyline series
of 1932–3. He was the only bowler ever to make Bradman appear
mortal, once striking the great man, as Larwood used to relate
with tight-mouthed glee, 'smack on the arse'. And just as he was
the principal weapon, so was he also the main victim of the affair,
as the Establishment closed ranks to protect the threatened
empire. Larwood was asked to apologise, refused, and never
played for England again.

The incident is perhaps the most sickening example of the
pernicious role that class prejudice has played in cricket. There are
many others – within living memory, working-class professionals
and gentleman amateurs had separate changing rooms, and even
walked to the wicket through different gates. Those ancient
distinctions were swept away in the relatively egalitarian sixties,
but, as the Authors' very own Ed Smith argues in his book *Luck*,
a new and more insidious form of unfairness has worked to
reinstate the old inequalities. Thirty years ago, Smith points out,
there was only one member of the England team touring Pakistan
who went to private school. Now, however, often three-quarters of
the England team are privately educated. It's a pattern replicated
in other sports – half the England rugby team and a disproportionate percentage of our Olympic medal winners also
attended fee-paying schools.

The reason is plain enough. And just in case we hadn't noticed, it was hammered home during the Authors' thrashing at the hands of the young gentlemen of Eton. Money buys superb facilities, top-quality coaching and the time and leisure to devote to perfecting that immaculate forward defensive, that textbook cover drive, that faintly condescending 'well played, hard luck'.

My own experience of school sport, at Corpus Christi High School in Leeds, was a little different. The school was one of the toughest in the city, squatting as it did in the midst of the run-down Halton Moor housing estate, then as now a byword for urban deprivation. PE was taught to us by a borderline psychotic Irishman called Frisco, who was convinced that cricket was anti-Irish, anti-Catholic, and almost certainly a gateway drug to the more outré reaches of sexual deviancy. Cricket coaching was limited to five minutes of Frisco yelling at us about personal hygiene, followed by a half-hour jog around the 'all-weather' sports pitch ('all-weather' in that it was equally unsuited to sporting activity in sunshine or rain, consisting, as it did, of an abrasive red gravel, designed to rasp away the flesh of a bare schoolboy leg like a microplane grater going through Parmesan).

Our school team played its home games a couple of miles away at the East Leeds cricket ground – perhaps the unloveliest in the country. Container lorries thundered along the A63 on one side, while on the other there was a desolate wasteland where you ran the twin risks of being stoned by gypsy children or dissolved in pools of industrial effluvia (the Leeds equivalents of Scylla and Charybdis). Beyond the sight-screen at the northern end lurked a slaughterhouse, and you'd often be accompanied, as you walked out to bat, by the screams of terrified pigs, the puzzled lowing of cattle, or the tragically misplaced optimism of the bleating sheep.

The team kitbag contained two ancient nut-brown bats, as cracked and wrinkled as a geriatric scrotum, along with four mismatched pads and three batting gloves of the rubber-spiked sort used by the hapless Australians against Larwood. During our very first match, back in the bleak (for this was Leeds, remember) summer of 1977, I was opening, drew the short straw and had to bat with a single glove. I was struck on the little fingernail in the first over. It remains my worst cricketing injury. After the game I showed my blackened nail to my mate Chris, who went straight into the centre of Leeds, shoplifted a pair of decent batting gloves from Lillywhites, and donated them to the team bag.

Back in Nottinghamshire, the Kirkby Portland ground couldn't match the squalor of East Leeds. (Kirkby Portland, I should say, took over the ground after the old Nuncargate village club folded in the late sixties.) In fact the ground is rather attractive, the outfield rising and falling in randomly undulating patterns, like buttocks at an orgy. Even the pylons and electricity lines marching across the fields afford a certain geometric aesthetic pleasure. There's a newish pavilion, not pretty perhaps, but functional, and good nets, and it all means that the club is thriving with plenty of promising youngsters coming through to keep the old lags on their toes.

And those old lags and young bucks were determined to give the southern softies in their boaters and cravats a lesson in how cricket gets played by real men, in the north.

And it's true that the Authors CC is crammed to the gills with the quite ludicrously posh. The tone is set by the skipper, Charlie. Splendid company, and a fine cricketer, one nevertheless suspects that there's an alternative universe in which he's standing amid the crenellations of a Gothic folly, drinking wine out of a cup formed from a human skull, a cruel smile playing over his lips as he contemplates the hanging of a peasant who failed to genuflect.

Besides Charlie, the team is packed with the full range of characters from a 1950s public school story – the hearty, sporty type; the etiolated intellectual; the endearingly modest earl; even an exiled Ruritanian princeling.

There are only three of us who went to state schools. There's Nick Hogg, a fine fast bowler, and the sort of batsman that has the cows in the next field huddling under the protective branches of a dying elm. His father, who played at this very ground forty years ago, is here to watch him. And then there's Jon Hotten, whose studious appearance belies both a working-class London background and a fondness for heavy metal. At forty-seven, Jon and I are also the most ancient of the regulars; we groan whenever we stand up or sit down, and have to nurse our creaking groins, our aged backs, and calves and hamstrings that manage to be both tight and flabby. Jon, however, has retained his lean and hungry look, whereas my strategy for fending off the ravages of time has been a sort of DIY collagen treatment – filling out the wrinkles with subcutaneous lard.

In some ways, Jon, Nick and I have more in common with the opposition than our own team. A few of the older Kirkby players had done their time in the pits. Most of the younger ones had gone off to uni, and so were in the middle of that same uncomfortable metamorphosis that I'd made, the one that transforms you from being working class into ... what? Something else. Something neither one thing nor the other.

But whatever our class allegiances, we were here to win a cricket match. And as this was the final game of the season, we all wanted to end on a high not purely powered by the local bitter.

It was a couple of the old boys who opened for Kirkby. Steve Richardson and Kevin Jones, former pitmen both, with a combined age of 112. The Authors made life tricky for them at the beginning. Matthew Parker has a classic fast bowler's snarl, and a visceral hatred of batsmen. He hasn't always come off for us this season, but today his wrath is focused, and two quick wickets are his reward.

It was as good as things were to get for the Authors. Richardson was joined by a youngster called Shead, and careful defence gave way to bludgeoning attack. Three figures were up, and the Authors were looking ragged.

Nick, our one truly high-class bowler, has a rare off day. Charlie is also below par. He's had a terrific season, not only captaining with panache, but making vital contributions with bat and ball. But he can't get it right today, and he goes for seven an over. Tom Holland, another generally solid performer with the ball this season, is hit out of the attack. I sense Charlie's eye flickering round the team. I perform some elaborate warming-up manoeuvres and it's enough to get the nod.

Although I went to school in Leeds, I was brought up, and learned my cricket outside the city, in Sherburn-in-Elmet in the West Riding of Yorkshire. After the pits and the fields, the biggest local employer was a huge meat processing plant, universally called the Bacon Factory, a place of Dantean torment where severed fingers and bodily fluids regularly found their way into pork pies and plastic pots of brawn.

The village team was a pretty fair cross-section of the local community, with a smattering of miners, various labourers and farmhands, a fellow who sniffed out dole cheats, a schoolteacher, even a moderately unsuccessful accountant or two.

I played for them from the age of fifteen. I was a decent cricketer back in those days, opening both the bowling and batting. However, I think the other guys always found it a little hard to get a grip on who or what I was. My parents – Scottish dad and Irish mum – weren't from the village, and I went off to my crappy school in Leeds rather than attending Sherburn High. That state of liminality – being betwixt and between, neither town nor country, not middle class, but not really working class either – is a fertile background for a writer, making you always an outsider, a watcher, something of a sneak; but it can also make for an awkward team-mate, and it took a particular incident to finally embed me into the side.

It occurred during the first game of the 1984 season. I came back across the Pennines from Manchester University to play in an away game at the almost stereotypically dour town of Mirfield. Getting changed before the game I realised that everyone else was staring at me. Or, rather, at my feet. I glanced down and saw that my toes were painted a glossy black. Too late I remembered that the night before, sitting alone in my room in halls, I'd taken a black marker pen and, for no very good reason other than ennui, coloured in my toenails, thinking I'd be able to wipe it off later, with a little spit. But the marker was permanent, and nothing shifted it.

'Fucking hell, McGowan,' said our captain, a collier and one-time bass guitarist with the terrible British heavy metal band Saxon, 'What are you studying at that university, the *Kama* bloody *Sutra*?'

From then on all was fine. It was official. I had a role. I was the club pervert. And I scored ninety-nine that day, although Mirfield beat us, as they usually did.

I loved my years playing for Sherburn, but my game never quite came on in the way it should have. I lost my nip, and then stopped bowling. With the bat I'd average in the mid-twenties each season. I'd win us the odd match with a blazing sixty or seventy, but never did beat that ninety-nine against Mirfield. Then, after university I moved down to London and more or less gave up cricket. I played a few games for the Civil Service, where I spent some years toiling as a hapless scribe, but it was no fun. I wasn't the team pervert. I wasn't the team anything.

And then, just as I thought I'd never play cricket again, I got the call from the Authors. A call that is, in the sense of hearing about the team from my friend Alex Preston, and then hurling myself on my arthritic knees before Charlie and begging to be let in, for one last chance of glory, of sporting redemption.

And now, here I was, ball in hand. I'd had a few overs already this season. I'd long abandoned trying to bowl fast, and instead

propelled looping off-spinners, that progressed so slowly the
opposition batsmen had time to change from their distance to
reading glasses to follow the flight.

I set my field.

'Everyone out.'

It was wise. That first over went for nine, although Charlie did
drop a chance at mid-on. It would have been my first wicket in
almost twenty years.

A less forgiving captain would have taken me off, but Charlie,
perhaps regretting that dropped catch, gave me another go. The
second over was a little better. Fourth ball up, I tried my solitary
variation – a slightly quicker ball propelled with a grunt like a gnu
giving birth. It bounced twice, and dribbled into the perplexed
batter's leg-stump.

Celebrations were short-lived. My third over went for another
nine, including a big six from Shead that landed just about where
Larwood used to start his run-up. Even Charlie's patience was
exhausted. Three overs. One for twenty-three.

In the end, despite an aggressive and controlled spell from Joe
Craig, and a tight one from twelve-year-old Ollie Parker
(Matthew's boy, and a very promising cricketer …) we were facing
a monumental 231.

A superb tea (they just do these things better in the north)
helped a little to assuage the pain. I know it always amuses the
paradoxically abstemious Hogg, but I feel if a nice lady has gone
to the effort of baking three different types of cake, then I should
go to the effort of eating three different types of cake …

One of the lessons of this season has been that, in general, if a
team bats well, they'll bowl well, so we were expecting a grim
battle. Much depended on our start. In Joe Craig and Sam Carter
we had two openers quite capable of getting us close. Sam has
been immense for us all season, at times seeming like Ajax slaying
sheep in his rage. Joe – a fellow children's writer – is the only

batsman in the team to touch Sam for brutality, but also has a certain panache and flourish that add an aesthetic delight to his strokes.

He gets a first-baller.

I'm batting three, and still buckling on my pads. I'd been hoping to see the scoreboard reading something like 140-1 at this stage. We're on ten.

I've had a rotten season with the bat. It hasn't helped that I've managed to run myself out half a dozen times. Raymond Queneau's *Exercises in Style* retells the same banal story in ninety-nine different ways. Similarly, I managed to illustrate almost all of the varied forms that a run-out can take: the overly casual second run; the carelessly ungrounded bat; the untied bootlace; chancing a run on a misfield; pausing midwicket to observe the flight of a skylark; the sly act of betrayal by one set upon my downfall. Well, not the last, sadly. They were all my fault, not least my tragic underestimation of the arm of an elfin young woman at Shepperton. My top score came back in my first innings, twenty-six against the Heartaches, but it had been downhill from there. I'd helped Sam put on about eighty against Hambledon, but my share was, I think, five. I was there at the end, but my eleven not out was perhaps the most hopeless innings of my life, consisting largely of the sort of pokes and prods you'd expect from a newly trained gynaecologist.

Part of the problem had been the pitches. Back in my heyday, I was a back-foot slasher. My driving has always been a bit hit and miss, but I was imperious with anything short. But we'd played all season on pitches that reminded me of the sort of quicksand Johnny Weissmuller would fall into, necessitating the summoning of a passing elephant with a cry of ungawa! ungawa! and a subsequent trunk-oriented rescue.

After a week or two without rain, the pitch at Kirkby was reasonably quick, if a little irregular in bounce. Larwood would have killed someone. I went out to face Jason Caunt, the Kirkby captain, a policeman by profession. Tall and awkward, he was as accurate as a fact checker on the *New Yorker*: I had to play at every ball, and there was nothing short enough to pull, nothing full enough to drive. Even Sam was subdued against him. By the end of his spell, Caunt had bowled five overs and taken 1-1, with four maidens.

Things were a little different at the other end. Dan Severn may not have been Harold Larwood, but he was the quickest bowler I'd faced all season. He whistled one past my nose in the first over I faced from him. Sam wandered down the wicket and said there was no shame in asking for a lid, but I've never worn a helmet and wasn't going to start now. The next ball was short again. I didn't have time to think. I moved back and across and hooked him down to long leg for four. It felt like the first real shot I'd played all year.

The next few overs from young Severn reminded me why I loved the game. I didn't have to ponder or wait or ruminate on the devils in the pitch or in my mind. Even my defensive shots were positive.

And I enjoyed the chat from the Kirkby guys. It wasn't sledging – they took the piss out of their own players more than us. But it was the kind of stuff that I remembered from my old days playing for Sherburn. Ancient in-jokes and newly minted one-liners flew around like late summer swallows. Mistakes were treated with mocking laughter, not snarls. After one delivery, a Kirkby old-timer yelled out to the bowler, 'you've got him walking into it now', meaning that my initial foot movement had been a little tentative, and I'd had to follow it up with a second, shuffling step. I got a good stride into the next ball, and looked around. He gave me the slightest hint of a nod. His comment had been meant as encouragement to the bowler but also, perhaps, as a coaching tip to me.

But my joy was not to last. They brought the quickie off (four overs for thirty), replacing him with the sort of innocuous trundler I'd been getting out to all season. I lost Sam, who failed, for once, to kick on after a start. It was my turn to try to force the pace, but all I did was to spoon a catch into the covers.

The Authors didn't put up much of a fight after that. Ben Falk looked good for a while; Jon Hotten proved his usual immovable self. Until, that is, he was moved. Hoggy swiped and slogged effectively, making his dad – a stylist, I was pretty sure, of the old school – wince a little. But we were all out for 101. It was our biggest defeat of the season.

Did it matter? Well, yes, it always matters when you lose. Your beer tastes flatter; the ache in the limbs is more intense; the drive home is longer. But ultimately the Authors' season wasn't so much about winning, as about *being*. Charlie and Nick had conjured us into existence, and that was a triumph in itself.

And here I was at forty-seven, playing again, and hooking a young buck into the long grass.

****

When I began to think about how I'd write about cricket and class, I thought I'd be angrier – more of a snarling Matthew Parker than a smiling Charlie Campbell. I planned to carp more about the inequalities that fracture and cripple our society, and the ways that those fracture lines carry on into the sporting world. And I thought I'd go in harder on the collection of toffs I was playing with.

But the truth is I just don't have the depth and weight of resentment or bitterness. My life has been too easy, my transition from the interzone between the working- and lower middle-class life to the other no-man's-land that is the place of the author, has been too smooth. And besides, I'd found that we all had our own class insecurities; none of us stood squarely, solidly rooted. I'd been happy at Corpus Christi; others in the team had been miserable at Eton. We were all partly outsiders, all watchers at the gates.

Cricket is a game unusually rich in metaphors. Jorge Luis Borges said in one of his Harvard lectures that the Chinese character representing 'the world' is more directly translated as 'the 10,000 things'. Had it truly been the case that the world contained merely 10,000 things, then the number of possible metaphors – taking a metaphor to be the bringing together of any two of those things – would be 99,990,000.

Now, clearly the world contains rather more than 10,000 things; and so, I expect, does cricket – Charlie has bought many of them from Millichamp & Hall. And this doubtless accounts for that metaphorical superabundance, from playing with a straight bat, to the sticky wicket; from keeping your end up, to being knocked for six.

But the most pervasive of cricketing metaphors is that which sees the game as representing society as a whole. It's a one-nation Tory kind of a view, in which the different strata of society – labourers and capitalists, or bowlers and batsmen – work together under the benign stewardship of the captain. The effort is individual, but the goals and the rewards are shared.

I'd reject this metaphor for two reasons. The first is that even if the best cricket teams are like that, society simply isn't. The interests of the rich and the poor are different. The wealthy want to keep their privileges, their tax breaks, and those schools with such wonderfully well-equipped sporting facilities; while the poor press their faces against the glass walls that keep them from the good stuff.

But that's not really why I reject the metaphor. I reject it because it does a disservice to cricket. Cricket should never be made to stand for anything outside itself. It remains a thing unique and precious. It is an engine for generating beauty and

tension and complexity and sorrow and joy. It is, to borrow
another Borgesian concept, the infinite library.

*This was our heaviest defeat of the season, at the hands of a
delightful side who were much too good for us. For some of us,
this was the last match of the summer. I managed to fit in a
couple more games, but Nick and I agreed that playing for
other teams just wasn't quite the same as turning out for the
Authors. We'd started the year almost as strangers, with only a
shared profession and love of cricket and we'd finished it with
the greatest team spirit I'd ever encountered. But then I, like
many of us, had spent the last decade not playing cricket, falling
victim to that old fallacy that talent was required.*

CRICKET AND REGRET:
AN ELEGY FOR A SEASON
Alex Preston

A cricket cap was on his head,
And his step seemed light and gay;
But I never saw a man who looked
So wistfully at the day.

Oscar Wilde, 'The Ballad of Reading Gaol'

First Innings

One summer in the middle years of the 1960s, an American friend of my grandfather went to Lord's with Samuel Beckett. Sitting under the black domes of their umbrellas in the stands, they watched a sheet of grey, wind-buffeted drizzle unfurl across the outfield. 'It always rains at cricket,' said Beckett. The two men sat in silence, my grandfather's friend puffing on the pipe that he had affected since moving to the UK. There was no play. They shuffled off to a pub in St John's Wood at half past two and sat looking out as the drizzle determined itself into rain. This, said my grandfather's friend, was a fine introduction to a particularly English sort of melancholy, and to cricket.

It is perhaps hackneyed to start my summary of the Authors' first season with a meteorological lamentation (isn't this what the Americans think we British do: play cricket and complain about the weather?) but when I close my eyes and think about the summer just gone, I picture a bruise-coloured sky lowering over a sodden infield, glum faces, drenched whites with mud-stained knees. I remember the sound of the first ball bowled at the Valley of Rocks, which hit the saturated wicket with the fricative plop of a pat dropped from the arse of a particularly tall cow. That we managed to play a book's worth of cricket this summer is a small miracle.

It was a summer of disappointment for me, and not just because of the weather. And yet, let us start with that weather. I remember, in late March, driving up to my mother-in-law's house in Shropshire. A day of bluebells and trilling birds, sunshine on blossom and leaf buds. Walking through woods with the dogs, we found ourselves in the grounds of the local stately home, Hardwick. There, on the square before the house, an ancient gardener pushed a rust-dappled roller across twenty-two yards of perfect spring wicket. A sudden thrill at the prospect of the summer ahead: to play at Arundel, Wormsley, Hambledon, Lord's … We were in the middle of a heatwave and – as is always the way – it felt as if the fine weather would last for ever. I'm not very good at hope, but there, for a brief moment, I was gloriously optimistic. I pictured fifties, gravity-defying catches, being carried on the shoulders of my team-mates. And always above us the strong hot beat of the sun.

Arundel, in fact, was rained off altogether – the days leading up to the game on 4 July felt torn from the pages of some sci-fi dystopia: dark storms chasing each other over the rooftops outside my study window, sudden howling squalls, hail showers pursued by rain so heavy the world disappeared, as if a curtain had been drawn across the windows from the outside. Arundel was my nearest proper cricket ground growing up and I remember sultry teenage days on picnic blankets, cider smuggled in thermoses, watching the match from the corners of our eyes, watching more closely our headmaster's nieces strolling along the far boundary, listening to the distant sound of bat on ball: the sound of a lollipop being pulled forcefully from a child's mouth. I spoke at a festival in Pulborough, not far from Arundel, two days after we were due to have played there. I felt like a politician visiting the scene of a natural disaster. Everything was still dripping, the people looked at my car as it passed with wild eyes above mud-streaked cheeks. When I stopped off at the cricket ground on the way home I saw that it was under several inches of water, a pair of mallards paddling importantly around mid-wicket.

When we did play, we often played in the rain. There is a particular skill to this: the ball keeps low; or it can slip from the bowler's hand and slant towards you at impossible angles. As Jon Hotten found to his cost, glasses become pearled with drizzle, creating for the wearer a prismatic vision of hundreds of possible cricket games, each suspended within its own drop of water. Nothing saps courage like cold English rain insinuating its way into the neck of your whites. From most of the Authors there was cheerfulness in the face of what seemed – to me at least – a bleak message from above, but as we sat steaming in pubs after those shower-sullied games we couldn't help feeling how unfair it all was. And the older sportsmen among us found themselves glancing at the clocks on the walls of those drinking establishments, aware of the relentless march of time, that the game we had just played was one more of their allotted share, that while some cricketers – Sir Tim Rice, for instance – carried on into their seventies, most of us would have the index finger raised on our careers in the coming years: ligament damage, shin splints, back pain. But more of death and decrepitude anon.

This chapter was supposed to be about Money and the Modern Game, you know. I wanted to write about Allen Stanford and the corruption that has come with the vast amounts of money funnelled into cricket over the past decade; the absurd circus of Lashings (the millionaire's play team based in Kent); I might have dropped in something about the time Deutsche Bank invited me to play at The Oval and I hit twenty runs off one Henry Olonga over; I would have recounted ball-by-ball blows of the game we were due to play against a team of bankers. In the end it didn't really come together (rather like my batting this summer).

We had a game pencilled in with an investment bank, but it was rained off. Later in the season I tried to rustle up a team of friends who worked in finance, but in the days leading up to the game the Federal Reserve announced a new round of quantitative easing and none of the bankers could get away from their desks. We ended up playing anyway, taking on a ragtag team of friends and distant acquaintances at a pitch in Dulwich. The closest we came to a banker was a pal of mine who was fired from Lehman Brothers several years ago.

In that game, as with so many others, my batting performance lurched from bad to out in a remarkably meagre number of balls. As a result of my all-too-brief stints at the crease, I spent a great deal of time this summer watching the Authors play. I'd sit on some likely bench or grass bank if it was sunny, more often finding myself cowering beneath an umbrella or in the shelter of the pavilion. I'd train my eyes on the field of play, feeling a bond of spectatorship with Ngayu, our photographer, as he perched on one perilous outcrop after another trying to capture a Sam pull shot at its explosive best, one of Charlie's imperious drives, an Amol cut so clinical it had Dr Thairu nodding in appreciation. As wicketkeeper, I also had the opportunity to observe us, caught as I was in the direct line of Nick's fizzing pace, Tom Holland's physics-laws-defying swing and Waheed Mirza's uniquely effective fast spin.

It's probably not something I should admit in a piece of writing that is likely to be read by O Captain! My Captain! but I spent a lot of time thinking out there behind the stumps. Such was the metronomic accuracy of our bowling attack that I was able to send my mind ranging off on extended divagations, to appreciate the wide-lens view of this late-in-life foray into the world of semi-professional cricket by a motley group of pensmen. I looked around at us – greying, paunchy, carrying beer-babies and curry-wings – and I felt a wash of sentiment at the sight. Cricket is the saddest sport, I think, something wistful in its very bones. And I'm sorry that this should be a downbeat note on which to end our tome, but cricket is a game all about endings and endings are sad: the brutal fall of the wicket; the end of partnerships that had seemed so settled, so sure; the rain sweeping all before it, necessitating the fiendish complexity of Duckworth–Lewis and early tea; the Chekhovian ending of the draw after a game in which not all that much has happened. And here we were, cricketers nearing the end of our playing lives, coming to the end of a summer of cricket, and the hope, the passion and the sheer professionalism with which we – to a man (and woman) – approached it was somehow heartbreaking.

Tea

During the tea break, we'll run through a reel of highlights, doing our best to pluck this digression from the maudlin trough into which it has stumbled. If you would, imagine some stirring music behind this montage: 'We Are the Champions', 'Eye of the Tiger' or 'The Ride of the Valkyries'. I need not include Tom Holland's six, since it feels like it has already seeded itself in the popular imagination with the repeated airing its author has given it on social media. Instead, we begin with Kamila's exemplary, controlled forward defensive shot against the ladies of Shepperton (testimony to the impeccable schooling provided by Waheed Mirza). Now picture Will contorting his body like Neo dodging bullets in *The Matrix* in order to take a catch of sublime athleticism at Wormsley (although was it this catch that led him to attempt the impossible dive at the Valley of Rocks, shattering his bones in the process?). Now we see Amol, leaping in the air, his face split in half by a grin, pumping his bat in the air to acknowledge his first ever fifty at Barkby (after a magnificent forty at Lord's). We come back to Will at Wormsley to applaud a cover drive of miraculous perfection. As the music darkens for a moment, watch a batting collapse of heartbreaking ineptitude against the Publishers; the music regains its spunk, and Sebastian and Jon lead a spirited fightback. We see Sam's ton at Hambledon, which won us the game. More shots of Sam playing with nerveless, stylish gusto, his schoolboy cap perched rakishly on golden locks. Nick's repeated bowling heroics. Tony's all-action style, stuffing his cap down the front of his trousers while fielding at short leg, and being run out every other game. The music stops. Tom Holland and Tom Penn engage in a poem-off (as they did between most overs), attempting to find in arcane Victorian verse a line capable of describing Charlie's inswinger or Matthew's yorker. The screen glows golden. The Authors in a pub in their whites after a game, laughing, drinking, triumphant, Laura and Ngayu, the genial spirits, accompanying us on our journey, crucial to our success. More golden glowing, some strings, perhaps. The picture fades.

Second Innings

It's no coincidence that earlier on Tom Holland described the sound of the fall of his wicket as a 'death rattle'. Every time I'm out, particularly if I'm bowled, it feels a little bit like dying. We're said to have had a 'decent innings' when we 'take the long walk back to the pavilion'. Comparisons between cricket and mortality have been made so often they've fallen into the realm of cliché. None of us expects that jag of late swing that finally carries us off. Wait! we cry, we haven't achieved half of what we'd dreamed we would! We wanted at least a five-wicket haul, a fifty, a six, a few more precious runs. The pause between the clatter of the stumps behind us and the sombre/satisfied rise of the umpire's finger contains within it the same mix of bewilderment, denial and resignation that we will feel in the seconds after the heart attack hits, the stroke strikes, the Transit van leaps the central reservation and bears down on our puny Nissan Micra.

Throughout the chapters in this book, there's an elegiac note, a sense of wistfulness surrounding our memories of cricket. If it is a game that lends itself to metaphors of mortality, it is also a game that seems preserved in the amber of our youth. Since – and I hope this doesn't upset anyone too much – there's already something archaic about cricket, a sense that it's too slow, too restrained a sport for a feverish, globalised modern world (hence the monstrous experiment that is Twenty20), it lends itself well to the sepia tones of memory. We mull nostalgically on the games of our childhood, where – again – the sun always seemed to shine and we had the vigour and chutzpah of youth to carry us to our Mike at Wrykyn-ish triumphs.

But now, from a perspective the wrong side of thirty, forty or, in some cases, fifty, we use cricket to mourn *eheu fugaces labuntur anni* ('alas the fleeting years pass away!'). Will's collarbone served as a powerful metonym for the fact that, in taking to the field with the seriousness and enthusiasm we did, looking to recapture the deathless joy of youth, we were found wanting. We, like Ned Merrill in John Cheever's 'The Swimmer', may still be compared to a summer's day, but only 'the last hours of one'. The dropped catches, the bellow-chested running between wickets, the air of tragedy when things didn't go our way: sometimes it was hard to watch.

I will end on an upbeat note, though. Go back and watch that tea-time montage again. Look at Sam sweeping the ball to the boundary, Amol swatting and smacking his way towards his fifty, Matthew and Nick and Tom bowling ball after hard-flung ball. Yes, we were fitter, better cricketers, more fearless, more attractive in our teens and twenties. Yes, there's something in our failures now that brings a lump to the throat, causes the sensitive to turn away with a mixture of pity and shame. But when we succeeded this summer, when we managed to turn back the clock and look – even for one ball – like the players we once were, how rich, how glorious a feeling. I scored seventy-six not out for Lancing College U15 against Christ's Hospital in 1994. My one, sweetly struck four this season gave me more pleasure than all those runs combined. We had thought our cricketing days behind us; they weren't, they aren't.

There is talk of future jaunts abroad for the Authors, whispers (so that our WAGs don't hear) that next year there will be more games, more chances to shine. Whatever, and despite the weather, this has been a golden summer. We leave it with new friends who already feel like old ones, bright memories, great hope.

All Out

EXTRAS

RAIN

Richard Beard

'Abandoned. Wet.'

So ends the story told by the scorecard from the Authors' last appearance at Lord's, in August 1912. Match abandoned is rarely a happy ending but at least the Authors, with Sir A. Conan Doyle opening the batting, managed a full innings. The luckless Publishers were cut short in their reply after seven overs: abandoned, wet. 'We had one of the most appalling summers ever known, even in England,' reported the editor of that season's *Wisden Cricketers' Almanack*, and no summer would be as damp for the next hundred years.

Until 2012, when the Authors CC re-formed.

Our climatic symmetry with the original Authors I find somehow reassuring, as if it means something. I may not be able to write as fluently as P. G. Wodehouse (in at number six, stumped for thirty-seven) nor defend with as straight a bat as Major F. G. Guggisberg (at four, author of *The Story of the Royal Military Academy*). I can, however, be rained on as proficiently as either. All cricketers have this experience in common – the rain was once as wet on the miniature cap and immense beard of W. G. Grace.

Cricketers need to respect the set of the weather. This is part of the game play, of the entertainment of match-day cricket. For an afternoon we escape whatever we are when not in whites, and cricket puts a deskbound writer back in touch with the natural world. With one eye on the clouds and the other on the Met Office weather app, we affect a feel for the wind and atmospheric pressure. For one day a week we're like farmers, or ancient mariners, our fate dependent on the weather.

In most cases when it rains, rain stops play. Rain is a catastrophe on weekends in the summer months of the year, but how wet is too wet for cricket? The measure I learned as a boy (when floods were no obvious deterrent) was that a square's fitness for cricket could be decided by an umpire's brogue. He puts one shoe inside the popping crease and leans his weight upon it. If water rises, the match is off. This method favours cricketers over groundsmen: it allows a pitch to be soft but playable. The match is on, the special wet-day rituals can begin.

Sawdust. There will be a poly bag of horribly compacted sawdust somewhere at the back of the tractor shed. The bowlers suck their teeth as they spread double handfuls over the unseasonably dark soil. The fielding captain frets over the state of the ball and out comes the cloth, usually a bar towel that ends up flapping from the band of the bowler's trousers. Before long the red of the ball is staining every player it touches.

The Authors' first match was scheduled for the end of April. Rain was forecast, and rain arrived. Fortunately, the East London Community CC had defences against the weather: they play on an artificial wicket in Victoria Park.

This is one area of technology where recreational cricketers have a genuine rainy-day advantage. Twenty-two yards of plastic can save a game. It also changes the game, the ball zipping off slicked Astroturf, then stopping dead in the grass of the saturated outfield. Hit high, hit long. Bowl fast.

Even then the rain will have its way. Twice the match was interrupted because, however beguiling cricket can be, there is an undeniable misery to standing for hours in a London park on a wet April Sunday. A huddle of cricketers took shelter under nearby trees. We looked for gaps in the solid grey cloud and agreed it could always be worse, and we were right. It could have been 1912.

These days the rain-affected pitch is rarely seen in televised cricket. Lord's has state-of-the-art drainage systems that could suck dry the Fens. Rain is a temporary inconvenience dismissed by hover-covers and super-soppers, countered mathematically with Duckworth and Lewis.

Rain at the cricket isn't what it used to be, but the unpredictable weather of the English summer, it seems to me, contributes to the existential attraction of the game. Sometimes, as a reminder of the great implacable universe, it rains and nothing can be done. Cricket is always played 'weather permitting' so the weather is never a background factor; it *participates*. It plays the role of Fate, and in 2012 the weather was greedy for a share of the action.

In the week before the club's long journey to Lynton & Lynmouth it rained every day. The fiction writers were prepared to suspend their disbelief – the match, they imagined, could feasibly take place. What will be will be. And after an epic drive to Devon's Valley of Rocks, ignoring every rational objection made by the team's historians, the Authors were rewarded with an unlikely but rainless Sunday. Fate was on our side.

Over the season the Authors' smart maroon caps were dampened in six out of fifteen fixtures. Another two were called off in advance, but only one game was abandoned entirely and never played, against the Arundel Castle Foundation XI at Arundel Castle. This, inevitably, would have been the Authors' finest hour. Runs would have been plundered, hat-tricks taken and miraculous catches plucked from the air. In the phantom

Arundel match, the game that got away, not one of the Authors failed.

A darkening of the clouds should sharpen a cricketer's appetite for the contest. Today might be the day. When the rain blows in, when the first heavy raindrops pock at dreams of glory, today would *definitely* have been the day. Definitely. The 2012 clouds, if I'm looking for a silver lining, will have channelled the optimism of cricketers everywhere. They left the perfect match unplayed, for at least another year.

STATISTICS

Andy Zaltzman

'Statistics,' as celebrity economist John Maynard Keynes himself once said, 'are like a ventriloquist's dummy – shove your hand far enough up them, and you can make them say whatever you want. But only children, and idiots, should take them at face value.'

Admittedly, Keynes said this off the record, to himself, while half-comatose after accidentally eating an absinthe-flavoured ice lolly on Skegness seafront, but the fiscal-stimulus fan nevertheless made a salient point, particularly in regard to cricket.

Statistics are an obsession shared by many cricket devotees, a comforting refuge of verifiable, documented facts in the ocean of barked opinion that is twenty-first-century discourse. They are also beloved by sports broadcasters, with increasing schedules and screen sizes to fill. Thirty years ago, televised cricket statistics seldom reached beyond a player's basic career numbers, which would be flashed up on screen, in the simplest conceivable font, when he walked out to bat. Now, the vast, wall-splattering acreage of the twenty-first-century goggle box, and twenty-four-hour-a-day coverage of sport, has led to an uncontrollable surge in the number of statistics power-hosed into our living rooms, regardless of whether or not they are illuminating, relevant or wildly misleading.

Traditional cricket statistics – averages, in particular – are becoming more and more meaningless. Test match figures have been skewed by players filling their boots against substandard teams, by an era of pudding pitches, bouncy bats and shorter boundaries, and by a mercilessly insistent global cricket calendar that often leaves teams exhausted, injured or as undercooked as a live piglet on a breakfast plate.

The commercial behemoth of Twenty20 has further muddied the statistical swamp. A player averaging fifty in Twenty20 cricket could be completely useless, if he is scoring his runs at three per over, while a team-mate averaging fifteen or twenty could be a regular match-winner. A bowler conceding eight runs per over might be a liability in the first ten overs of a T20 match, but a genius in the final five. T20 has yet to develop a meaningful method of measuring performance that is not preceded by a dollar sign.

Viv Richards was voted one of the five Cricketers of the Twentieth Century by *Wisden*'s hundred-strong panel of experts from all corners of the universe. His Test average was a fraction over fifty – outstanding, but only the twenty-second best Test batting average of the century (of players who played twenty Tests or more). Admittedly, Richards was also probably the best one-day-international batsman in the history of the shorter format. And the most impressive gum-chewer the game has seen. And had the finest strut in world sport. And was a sporting and cultural icon of such supernatural coolness that he could have sunk the *Titanic* just by looking at it. And, above all, he batted how Zeus would have batted if he had been a cricketer instead of a (probably) fictional ancient Greek megagod. Judged purely on the distracting siren of career Test average, however, he was a worse batsman than

Thilan Samaraweera. The Sri Lankan's Test average is currently fifty. He is a fine batsman, a late-flowering craftsman who has scored hundreds against all the other Test nations bar Australia. But even his mother would not claim he is a better batsman than Viv Richards.

The Authors' 2012 season averages, however, leave little room for dispute, by the players or their doting parents. Novelist Nicholas Hogg dominated the bowling figures, taking twenty-nine wickets at an average of seventeen, an almost Richard Hadlee-esque superiority over his grateful team-mates. Sam Carter, while by no means the most prolific author of the Authors – as an editor, he has been the midwife of books, rather than their mother, and, according to rumour, qualified for the team under ICC laws thanks to a grandfather who once wrote a best-selling pamphlet about how to cook ferrets – was its most prolific batsman, by a country mile, and an extremely rural country mile at that, lined with verdant hedgerows, angry badgers and a lingering sense of resentment about the Industrial Revolution.

No one would dispute that Sam was the team's foremost batsman, scoring almost three times as many runs as the next highest run-maker. He himself will no doubt be eternally delighted that he averaged more than twice as much as former Test batsman Ed Smith. Albeit that Ed played only one match, so his 'average' of twenty-four has as much meaning as Garfield Sobers' one-day-international batting average of 0.00. From one match. It is fair to assume that, had Sobers been playing today, his one-day average would have been significantly higher, and his IPL contract would be worth more than the GDP of some medium-sized countries. Nevertheless, in the 2012 Authors CC season, Sam Carter (Oundle School 3rd XI, Newick CC, Sussex Martlets & any other team in need of a spare player) was almost twice as good a batsman as Ed Smith (Cambridge University, Kent, Middlesex & England). That is a stone-cold fact. Thanks be to stats. Amen.

Back to Viv Richards. When the Beethoven of Batsmanship walked out to bat for his final Test innings at The Oval in 1991, he needed twenty runs to ensure he ended with a career average of fifty. There was widespread relief that he passed this curious statistical milestone, as if he would have been a lesser player had he averaged 49.99 as opposed to 50.01. Would he have been voted one of the five best cricketers of the controversial twentieth century if he had failed in that final innings, with an average humiliatingly cowering a meaningless fraction below the half-century mark? Perhaps. Perhaps not. Would the memory of him at his peerlessly majestic peak have been retrospectively dulled by the fact that, after a decline in his late thirties, he did not average fifty, so could not have been as good as he was cracked up to be? No. Not unless the person doing the remembering is a certifiable buffoon.

This is not to suggest that cricket's traditional statistics, with their focus on achievement rather than impact, are without any worth or meaning. But their worth and meaning sometimes require considerable coaxing out into the open. Cricket has never generated the same range of relevant, enlightening numbers as its rogue American cousin baseball, which breeds stats like Catholic rabbits. Baseball is a more scientifically measurable sport.

Cricket's numbers, however, if they are to have any relevance beyond filling an awkward space on the TV screen, or in a book, or in an attempted seduction, demand to be interpreted like the entrails of a Babylonian sheep, gymnastically contorted to reveal their true form, cross-examined in a darkened cell without a lawyer present, or selectively ignored. As Mrs Samaraweera would no doubt vociferously testify as she settles down to watch an old video of King Viv hitting 291 at the Oval in 1976.

PLAYER BIOGRAPHIES

The following played for the Authors this season and contributed to this book:

Richard Beard is a novelist, non-fiction writer and Director of the National Academy of Writing. He is vice captain of Clifton Hampden Cricket Club.

Charlie Campbell is captain of the Authors XI. Off the pitch, he is a literary agent and the author of *Scapegoat: A History of Blaming Other People*. This was his first season as captain of any sporting side.

Sam Carter is Editorial Director of Biteback Publishing. Born in London, he spent most of his childhood in East Sussex and still plays much of his cricket there for Newick CC and the Sussex Martlets. He read Modern History at University College, Oxford, and has enjoyed a career in London publishing, tinkering with fiction and non-fiction of all genres, after a happy decision to call time on a law career.

Sebastian Faulks has written more books than anyone can remember. They include *A Possible Life*, *Human Traces*, *The Fatal Englishman* and *Birdsong*. He first picked up a cricket bat when Peter May was England captain, though for some reason they never batted together; he does, however, claim to have thick-edged Gary Sobers for four in a charity match in 1990. He likes to shape the Authors' innings from the pivotal number nine position and, of necessity, to field close to the wicket.

William Fiennes is the author of *The Snow Geese* and *The Music Room*, and co-founder of the charity First Story, which promotes writing in secondary schools.

Peter Frankopan divides his time between being an Oxford don, an international hotelier and President of the Croatian Cricket Federation. He is author of *The First Crusade: The Call from the East* and has translated *The Alexiad* for Penguin Classics. Having played tennis with Tim Henman at Wimbledon, and with Blues from both Oxford and Cambridge, his appearance for the Authors XI at Lord's in the 2012 season completes another leg of a personal sporting Grand Slam.

Nicholas Hogg is the author of two novels, *Show Me the Sky* and *The Hummingbird and the Bear*. He has won numerous short story prizes, including the Bridport, Raymond Carver and New Writing Ventures contests, and his work has also been broadcast by the BBC. A Leicestershire Schools and County U19 player, he claims once to have trapped Chris Broad plumb lbw in a match at Grace Road – not that the umpire agreed with him.

James Holland is a historian of the Second World War, whose books include the bestselling *Battle of Britain* and *Dam Busters*. He has written a number of wartime novels and has written and presented several BAFTA-shortlisted films for the BBC. He has also lectured to the MCC at Lord's.

Tom Holland is a prize-winning historian, whose books – *Rubicon*, *Persian Fire*, *Millennium* and *In the Shadow of the Sword* – cover the rise and fall of ancient empires. He has made documentaries for both the BBC and Channel 4, and presents Radio 4's *Making History*. His translation of Herodotus will be published by Penguin Classics in 2013. His first six, hit while playing for the Authors XI, has become a Twitter sensation and has already featured in the *Evening Standard* and Radio 4's *Front Row* as one of the big sporting stories of the summer of 2012.

Jon Hotten is the author of *Muscle* and *The Years of the Locust* and writes the popular cricket blog, The Old Batsman.

Anthony McGowan is a multi-award-winning author of books for adults, teenagers and younger children. He was born in Manchester, brought up in Yorkshire, and lives in London. The film of his YA novel, *The Knife that Killed Me*, is out in 2013. Once a dashing opening batsman and snaking outswing bowler, he now propels gentle off spin, and longs only to top the 99 he scored against Mirfield in the West Riding League in 1984.

Matthew Parker is a historian who now bowls almost as slowly as he writes and he would love to be faster at both. He is the author of *Monte Cassino*, *Hell's Gorge* and most recently *The Sugar Barons*.

Thomas Penn is the author of *Winter King: The Dawn of Tudor England*. He holds a PhD in medieval history from Clare College, Cambridge. He writes for, among others, the *Guardian*, the *Daily Telegraph* and the *London Review of Books*.

Alex Preston is the bestselling author of *This Bleeding City* and *The Revelations*. He is a regular panellist on BBC2's *The Review Show* and Radio 4's *Saturday Review*. His next novel has a section charting high-octane cricketing adventures in war-torn Europe.

Amol Rajan is Editor of the *Independent*, a columnist for the *Evening Standard*, and author of *Twirlymen: The Unlikely History of Cricket's Greatest Spin Bowlers*.

Kamila Shamsie has written five novels including *Burnt Shadows* which was shortlisted for the Orange Prize and translated into more than twenty languages. She grew up in Karachi watching cricket, but not playing it. The Authors XI changed that.

Ed Smith is an author, journalist and broadcaster. He was formerly a professional cricketer for Kent, Middlesex and England. His most recent book is *Luck: A Fresh Look At Fortune*.

Dan Stevens, while an aspiring author, is really an actor, best known for playing Matthew Crawley in the ITV series *Downton Abbey*. He is Editor-at-Large for the online quarterly *The Junket*, publishes a regular column in the *Sunday Telegraph*, and was a judge on the panel of the 2012 Man Booker Prize. Cricket is not his first language.

Andy Zaltzman is the co-star of the global hit satirical podcast *The Bugle*. He has appeared on several Radio 4 shows, stars alongside Al Murray on *7 Day Sunday* on 5 Live, and can be seen very sporadically on television. He writes The Confectionery Stall blog for ESPNCricinfo.com, and in 2008 wrote his first book, *Does Anything Eat Bankers?*, a comedic response to the credit crunch, in a bold effort to claim the prestigious Most Infantile Tome Ever Written About Economics title. A regular performer at the

Edinburgh Fringe, Andy has also sold out stand-up shows in London, New York and Bangladesh. Yes, Bangladesh.

The following writers also turned out for the Authors XI in 2012: Jonathan Beckman, bowler, senior editor at *Literary Review* and author of *Marie Antoinette and the Necklace Scandal*; Joe Craig, opening batsman and author of the Jimmy Coates series for young adults; Ben Falk, all-rounder, journalist and biographer; Ed Howker, batsman, journalist and co-author of *Jilted Generation*; Mirza Waheed, bowler of astonishing variety and guile, and author of *The Collaborator*; Pankaj Mishra, all-rounder, essayist and author of *From the Ruins of Empire*; Dave Rear, bowler, academic and author of *A Less Boring History of the World*; William Sutton, author of *The Worms of Euston Square*, batsman and former Brazil international; Tom Vowler, novelist and preternaturally youthful all-rounder.

ACKNOWLEDGEMENTS

The Authors received tremendous support and assistance over the course of the season and in the writing of this book. Firstly, we would like to thank the clubs and teams who made the summer of 2012 such an utter joy: the East London Community CC, the Heartaches CC, the Bushmen CC, the Lords and Commons CC, the Eton 3rd XI, Millichamp & Hall's XI, Shepperton Ladies, Lynton & Lynmouth CC, the Thespian Thunderers, Hambledon CC, the Publishers, the Gaieties CC, Barkby United CC and Kirkby Portland CC. We are also very grateful to Tim Munton and Mark Foster at Wormsley, to Debbie Moore, Sara Hales, Neil Robinson and all at the MCC, to Tim Beard and his colleagues at Eton, to Chalke Valley CC, to Dulwich College and to John Barclay. Thanks also to John Betts, Peter King, Gordon Robinson and Richard Miller for their excellent umpiring skills, to Darren Maddy and Neil Carter for their generosity and coaching skills and to Gunn & Moore.

Over the season, we raised money for two very fine charities – First Story and Chance to Shine, which promote creative writing and cricket respectively in state schools. We were incredibly fortunate to be sponsored by Christie's, which allowed us to support these causes effectively. We would like to thank Steven Murphy, Katy Richards, Zita Gibson and their colleagues for all their help and generosity. Thanks also to Katie Waldegrave and Kirstie Miller at First Story and Claire Hall at Chance to Shine, to the estate of P. G. Wodehouse, and to Hadley Freeman, Joy Lo Dico, Daniel Norcross, Matt Thacker, Huw Turbervill, Katie Walker, and Ellie Bury, Ella-mai Robey and John Wilson at *Front Row* for their effusive coverage of our distinctly average sporting team. And we are very grateful to Tristan Jones for his editorial expertise, to Digvijay Kathiwada and Osian's CC for our website and much else and to Ned Cranborne for his hospitality.

On the publishing front, we would like to thank Charlotte Atyeo, Nick Humphrey, Ellen Williams, Richard Charkin and all at Bloomsbury for their brilliant hard work on our book. The team around the team could not have been better. Which brings me to our final thanks: to our valiant photographer Ngayu Thairu and our wonderful scorer Laura Jeffrey, who recorded our season so beautifully. Laura also organised the Authors' first ever tour abroad, which Ngayu accompanied us on too. But that is a whole other story.